THE DIMENSIONS THAT ESTABLISH AND SUSTAIN RELIGIOUS IDENTITY

THE DIMENSIONS THAT ESTABLISH AND SUSTAIN RELIGIOUS IDENTITY

A Study of Chinese Singaporeans Who are Buddhists or Taoists

Daniel H. Y. Low

Foreword by Chung Kwang Tung

WIPF & STOCK · Eugene, Oregon

THE DIMENSIONS THAT ESTABLISH AND SUSTAIN RELIGIOUS IDENTITY
A Study of Chinese Singaporeans Who are Buddhists or Taoists

Copyright © 2018 Daniel H. Y. Low. All rights reserved. Except for brief quotations in critical publications or reviews, no part of this book may be reproduced in any manner without prior written permission from the publisher. Write: Permissions, Wipf and Stock Publishers, 199 W. 8th Ave., Suite 3, Eugene, OR 97401.

Wipf & Stock
An Imprint of Wipf and Stock Publishers
199 W. 8th Ave., Suite 3
Eugene, OR 97401

www.wipfandstock.com

PAPERBACK ISBN: 978-1-5326-1812-3
HARDCOVER ISBN: 978-1-4982-4341-4
EBOOK ISBN: 978-1-4982-4340-7

Manufactured in the U.S.A.

For Melody & the rest of the M*s*—
Megan, Malcolm, Meryl, Mitchell, Meredith.

Contents

List of Figures | xi
List of Tables | xii
Foreword | xiii
Preface | xv
Acknowledgments | xvii

Chapter 1. Introduction | 1
    Rationale for Research | 6
    Purpose of Research | 6
    Definition of Terms | 7
    Scope of Research | 9
    Limitations of Research | 10
    Significance of Research | 11

Chapter 2. Review of Studies on Buddhism and Taoism and Religious Identity in Singapore | 13
    An Overview of Singapore's Chinese Community and its Religious Practices | 14
    Pre-independence Period | 14
        Taoism/folk religion | 15
        Buddhism/Chinese Buddhism | 17
    Post-independence Period | 18
    Studies on Buddhism and Taoism in Singapore | 20
        General Accounts of Buddhism and Taoism | 20
        Sociological Studies on Buddhism and Taoism | 22
        Historical Studies on Buddhism and Taoism | 30
    Discussion | 32

Contents

Chapter 3. Review of Theories of Identity and Religious Identity | 36
    An Overview of Theories of Identity and Identity Formation | 38
        Early Development | 38
            Erik Erikson | 38
            James E. Marcia | 40
        Later Development | 41
            Identity Theory | 41
            Social Identity Theory | 44
    Studies on Religious Identity and Religion's Impact on Identity | 46
    Discussion | 51
    Summary of Review | 55

Chapter 4. Research Methods and Procedures | 56
    Reasons for Qualitative Research | 56
        Nature and Context of the Research Topic | 56
        Underlying Philosophical Assumptions | 57
            Personal Background | 58
            Personal Philosophical Assumptions | 58
            Ontology | 58
            Epistemology | 60
            Axiology | 60
            Rhetoric | 61
            Method | 61
            Role of Researcher | 62
            Interpretive Paradigms | 63
    Reasons for Grounded Theory | 64
        Sampling Procedure in Grounded Theory | 64
        Sampling Criteria and Participants in Grounded Theory | 65
    Data Collection | 66
        Data Collection: Interviews | 66
        Data Collection: Observations | 66
        Literature Review and Use of Literature | 67
    Time Frame, Length, and Number of Interviews, Locations, and Protocol | 68
        Ethical Considerations | 68
        Data Validation and Verification | 68
            Triangulation | 69

CONTENTS

    Member Checks | 69
    Peer Review | 70
    Reflexivity | 70
    Rich and Thick Description | 70
    Audit Trail | 70
    Adequate Engagement in Data Collection/
    Saturation | 71
Discussion | 71

Chapter 5. Emerging Domain: Recognition | 72
  Analysis of Data | 72
  Recognition of the Enfolding Presence and Power of Spiritual
  Realities | 81
    Participation | 81
      Family | 81
      Friends | 82
    Revelation | 87
      Destiny | 88
      Manifestation | 90
  Discussion | 99

Chapter 6. Emerging Domain: Appreciation | 101
  Appreciation of the Enfolding Presence and Power of Spiritual
  Realities | 103
    Transformation | 103
      Overcoming Personal Crisis | 103
      Renewing Negative aAttitudes | 105
    Direction | 108
      Insights | 108
      Ethics | 110
    Protection | 114
      Daily Protection | 115
      Special Protection | 116
    Appreciation via Disagreement | 117
      Insensitivity | 118
      Inconsistency | 121
  Discussion | 122

Contents

Chapter 7. Emerging Domain: Dedication | 124
    Dedication to the Enfolding Presence and Power of Spiritual Realities | 125
        Aspiration | 125
            Personal-oriented | 125
            Others-oriented | 129
        Obligation | 132
            Present Life | 133
            After Life | 137
    Discussion | 139

Chapter 8. The Centrality of Spiritual Realities in Religious Identity | 140
    The Enfolding Presence and Power of Spiritual Realities in Establishing and Sustaining Religious Identity | 142
        Recognition | 143
        Appreciation | 144
        Dedication | 145
    Implications of Study | 146
        Implications for Research | 146
            Participants | 146
            Research in Singapore | 147
            Research in Theories of Identity and Religious Identity | 148
        Implications for Practice | 149
    Recommendations for Further Study | 152
    Conclusion | 153

Appendix—Sample Interview Guide | 157
Bibliography | 159

Figures

1. A model of the enfolding presence and power of spiritual realities in establishing and sustaining the religious identity of Chinese Singaporeans who are Buddhists or Taoists | 75

Tables

1. Demographic data of participants | 73

Foreword

Singapore's religious landscape consists of diverse representation of almost every major religious tradition. Over the last two decades, Buddhism and Taoism have experienced and continue to witness revitalization such that they have the highest number of adherents within the Chinese population. Daniel Low's study, along with the grounded theory that he has developed, is timely in the following ways.

First, the voices of the participants add robustness to the dimensions that sustain religious identity—addressing the gaps that continue to exist from research dominated by Western research. At the same time, people of other ethnic and/or religious backgrounds gain a deeper understanding of the spiritual realities that surround Chinese Singaporeans who are Buddhists or Taoists.

There is a lack of studies related to Chinese religions emerging from Singapore. I am hopeful that this publication will spur further local research to provide fresh insights into the varied contributions of ancient religions in a modern and secular state.

Master Chung Kwang Tong (Wei Yi)
Taoist Priest
Singapore

Preface

Amidst Singapore's rapid pace of modernization and globalization, the practices and rituals associated with the traditional Chinese religions of Buddhism and Taoism remain prominent on the island and vibrant among the majority of Chinese Singaporeans. Buddhism and Taoism continue to be the dominant religions, with their adherents making up more than half of the island's population. Previous studies that have emerged from Singapore point out that the persistent dominance and vibrancy of these religions reflect the enduring strength of the adherents' religious identity or identification.

Despite the increasing prominence of utilizing the term "religious identity," these studies have done little to provide any theoretical precision for the term and to help understand the dimensions that establish and sustain it within the daily experiences of the adherents. The purpose of this study is to discover and explain the dimensions that establish and sustain the religious identity of Chinese Singaporeans who are either Buddhists or Taoists, with religious identity being reconceptualized to encompass the critical and inherent characteristics within the two overlapping entities that undergird the term—i.e. religion and identity.

Through a qualitative approach, data was collected via face-to-face interviews and observations in Singapore to discover and explain the dimensions that the participants articulated as significant in their continued commitment as Buddhists or Taoists. Subsequently, the data was analyzed through the Grounded Theory method. The theory that emerged—*The Enfolding Presence and Power of Spiritual Realities*—proposes that the participants' religious identity as either Buddhist or Taoist is established and sustained as they come to recognize, appreciate, and dedicate themselves to these realities.

Preface

This study, together with the emergent theory, is significant in a number of ways. First, it provides a more nuanced and robust understanding of the varied features that undergird religious identity within the current academic discourse on religion and religious identity that has emerged from Singapore. Second, it generates useful insights to address the existing gaps within the broader investigation of religious identity that have largely been dominated by studies from the West. Finally, it furnishes other religious communities in Singapore with resources to strengthen future interreligious interactions and understanding.

Acknowledgments

My doctoral journey (2009–2014), which culminated in the successful defense and now publication of this research, would be impossible without the collective effort of the following people in my life:

1. Melody: Best friend, wife, and mother to our five lovely children. Her unconditional self-sacrifice and love, along with constant encouragement, prayers, and reminders of what matters in life, enabled me to focus and complete the program in a timely manner. To her I owe my greatest debt!

2. Megan, Malcolm, Meryl, Mitchell, and Meredith: Each of them—with their unique gifts and personalities and constant presence—added precious and memorable dimensions to this journey. Their laughter, hugs, and jokes never failed to warm my heart and strengthened me throughout the journey!

3. My parents and parents-in-law: Their support, love, and encouragement in a variety of ways and regular visits have blessed the years we have been in the United States. May they continue to experience the Lord's care and strength!

4. Drs. Rhonda McEwen, Stephanie Chan, and Russell Bowers, Jr: As committee members and faculty, they demanded the very best and unselfishly shared their wisdom, insights, and time! As friends, they prayed for and encouraged my family and I. I am honored to call them teachers and friends!

5. Faculty and Friends at Cook School of Intercultural Studies and Biola University: Each of you—Drs. Michael Lessard-Clouston, Rich Starcher, and Leanne Dzubinski; Ivan Chung, Andrew Yee, Skip Stare, Sakunee Kriangchaiporn, David Ofumbi, Claudia Canales, and peers

Acknowledgments

at the Doctoral Research Group (DRG)—have walked and/or collaborated with me over the course of six years. I treasure your friendship and the dialogues we have had over a spectrum of topics.

CHAPTER 1

INTRODUCTION

SINGAPORE HAS EXPERIENCED RAPID modernization and globalization over the last fifty years, morphing from a third-world country into a developed nation in a relatively short time. Despite significant economic progress and social changes within this secular state, the variety and vibrancy of age-old practices and rituals associated with the traditional Chinese religions of Buddhism and Taoism continue to feature prominently across Singapore's social landscape.

These emotion-evoking and oft-repeated actions consist of both the highly formalized and less formal. Examples of the highly formalized ones include Taking Refuge in the Triple Gems—the Buddha, the Dharma and, the Sangha—inviting Buddhist monks or Taoist priests to perform the final rites for their deceased members, and participating annually in the physically demanding 三步一拜 (*san bu yi bai,* or Three-Step-One-Bow) ceremonies held at many Buddhist temples during Vesak Day. The less formal ones include individuals or families setting up makeshift 坛 (*tan,* or altars) at home, places of work, or along walkways filled with canned and freshly prepared food, and accompanied by candles, joss sticks, and large urns for the burning of 金纸 (*jin zhi,* golden paper or "hell notes") during the Lunar Seventh Month; practicing the values prescribed by the Five Precepts, Eight-fold Path or 道德经 (*Dao de jing,* or Classic of The Way and Virtue); meditating or chanting alongside *kalyana mitras* (spiritual friends) with the help of *suttas*; and the daily offering of joss sticks before various family gods, such as 观音菩萨 (*Guan yin pu sa,* or Bodhisattva Guan yin), 大伯公 (*Da bo gong,* or Grand Uncle), 关帝 (*Guan di,* also known as God of

War), or 齐天大圣 (*Qi tian da sheng*, Great Sage Equal of Heaven, or, more commonly, the Monkey God).

While the prominence of these vibrant practices and rituals is to be expected, given that the number of Buddhists and Taoists constitute more than half of the island's population and Buddhism and Taoism continue to be the religions of choice for the majority of Chinese Singaporeans, what are the plausible explanations for the persistent practice of these traditional religions in modern Singapore? How do Buddhists and Taoists remain lifelong adherents even as the island rapidly transforms due to the exponential growth of cutting edge and high value-added industries (e.g. petrochemicals, life sciences, and precision engineering) and the government's relentless push for the island to be a Smart Nation?

Scholarly studies that have emerged from Singapore and explored this phenomenon point to the enduring and renewed strength of the Buddhists' and Taoists' religious identity or religious identification.[1] This strength is often attributed to effectiveness in processes of religious modernization and changes undertaken by these two religions, which include rationalization and intellectualization, so much so that both continue to attract new adherents.[2] At the same time, such strength has also been linked to the close affinity between religious identity and ethnic identity, i.e., Chinese Singaporeans, particularly those who use predominantly Mandarin or Chinese dialects, accordingly practice the Chinese traditional religions of Buddhism, Taoism, or an amalgamated form of both.[3]

Although these studies are undoubtedly valuable in shedding insight into the significant and sustained impact of Buddhism and Taoism on the lives of many Chinese Singaporeans, they have failed to fully account for what establishes and sustains the religious identity of the Buddhists and Taoists and how religious identity is defined and understood. While the gaps in these studies will be further explored in chapter 2, it is sufficient at this juncture to provide an overview of the key issues and how this study proposes to address these issues.

First, although many of the existing studies are peppered with the use of "religious identity" as a term, these studies have not attempted to give the term any theoretical precision. It is often used either conjointly with social

---

1. Lai, "Introduction," xliii; Tan, "Keeping God in Place," 56, 58.
2. Kuah-Pearce, *State, Society, and Religious Engineering*; Tong, *Rationalizing Religion*, 3–5; Choong, "Religious Composition of the Chinese," 334.
3. Goh, "Chinese Religion and the Challenge," 108.

INTRODUCTION

or racial identity or group category[4] or synonymously with closely associated terms such as "religious identification" or "religiosity."[5] Yet, religious identity is a unique component within an individual's identity that encompasses the important characteristics embedded within the overlapping but distinct entities of identity and religion.[6] These characteristics include, within the entity of identity, an inherent sense of invigorating continuity and well-being amidst the various transformations experienced by an individual such that identity functions as a personal code or referent system.[7] Within the entity of religion, the key characteristics include experiences with one or more of the following metaphysical or divine realities: sacred beings, texts, community, and actions or forms.[8]

Thus, its use should be differentiated from religious identification, which is essentially a process undertaken by an individual to connect with "others in an organizational sense (as in becoming a formal member) or in a symbolic sense (as in thinking of oneself as part of a particular group)."[9] At the same time, religious identity should also be differentiated from religiosity, as religiosity is largely viewed as "ways of being religious"[10] or expressions of one's beliefs (e.g., religious participation).

With the continued and pervasive importance of Buddhism and Taoism among Chinese Singaporeans, this study proposes that religious identity be adopted as an analytical construct in light of the unique characteristics pointed out above in order to discover and explain the dimensions that undergird Chinese Singaporeans' choice to remain as Buddhists or Taoists. Religious identity will be defined as an individual's awareness of and commitment to: (a) a continuous and invigorating inner well-being and (b) a sense of belonging and desire to extend the well-being to the sociocultural community associated with the divine. The awareness and commitment arise out of an individual's reciprocal interactions with the divine and the

---

4. Tan, "Creating 'Good Citizens,'" 133. See also Xu, "Daoist Temples in Modern City Life," 131.

5. Lai, "Introduction," xliii and xlvi; Tong, *Rationalizing Religion*, 177, 266.

6. Bell, "Religious Identity," 10.

7. Dashefsky, "And the Search Goes On," 240. See also Berger, "Modern Identity," 167–68; Erikson, *Identity*, 19; King, "Religion and Identity," 197; Kohn and Roth, "Introduction," 1–3; Mol, *Identity and the Sacred*, 65.

8. Berger, *Sacred Canopy*, 29–51; Ching, *Chinese Religions*, 11; Erikson, *Identity and the Life Cycle*, 67; Mitchell, *Buddhism*, 2.

9. Dashefsky, "And the Search Goes On," 242.

10. Berkel et al., "Similarities and Differences," 4.

sociocultural community associated with the divine. The incorporation of these characteristics is in line with Gleason's call for a more responsible use of the concept, where the intrinsic complexities of the subject matter are taken into account.[11]

The unabated importance and renewed flourishing of Buddhism and Taoism in Singapore, even gaining converts from Chinese Singaporeans who are educated in institutions of higher learning, have ensured that both religions continue to have the largest following.[12] Yet much remains unknown as to what the Buddhists and Taoists will highlight as the dimensions that establish and sustain their religious identity. Do the metaphysical or divine constituents inherent in these religions have a role to play? And if so, how will the adherents describe this role? How do sacred texts, community, and actions contribute to the sense of wholeness experienced by the adherents?

Second, the impact of conjoining religious identity with social identity or group category in current research has resulted in an overemphasis on external factors, such as societal and structural or environmental forces (e.g., Chinese community, government policies, processes to modernize undertaken by Buddhist and Taoist organizations), as the primary dimensions that establish and sustain religious identity. For example, most of the studies on Buddhism in Singapore have focused heavily on tracing the religion's structural transformations, and thus provide a limited perspective on the embedded multifaceted dimensions that make it meaningful for its adherents.

Similarly for studies into Taoism, while far fewer than Buddhism and often subsumed with the latter, these have also adopted a macro-perspective approach. They focus on topics such as organizational transformations,[13] continued adherence to religion due to pride in "membership of a great body of tradition"[14] as Chinese, the reformation of the religion via "rationalization" and "intellectualization,"[15] and transfiguration (i.e., change in meaning without a change in form) or hybridization (i.e., change in form without a change in meaning) or transfiguring hybridity (i.e., the overlap of transfiguration

---

11. Gleason, "Identifying Identity," 931.

12. Singapore Department of Statistics, *Census of Population 2000* and *Census of Population 2010*; Yen, "Taoists and Buddhists still Biggest Group."

13. Sinha, "'Hinduism' and 'Taoism' in Singapore," 137–38. Also, Xu, "Daoist Temples in Modern City Life," 131.

14. Clammer, "Chinese Ethnicity and Political Culture," 280.

15. Tham, "Religious Influences and Impulses," 23; Tong, *Rationalizing Religion*, 4, 6.

INTRODUCTION

and hybridization) due to the inherent dynamism found within the Taoism or Buddhism that enable them to create new meanings or practices.[16]

Thus, the utilization of this broadened conceptualization of religious identity as an analytical construct offers a fresh approach to explore why many Chinese Singaporeans continue to adhere or turn to Buddhism or Taoism. It provides an impetus to look beyond the macro-perspective approach of labeling external changes or environmental forces as being the key explanations for the adherents' strong religious identity. It also sensitizes research to the spiritual entities existing within Buddhism and Taoism's "world and realities which offer motivations, fulfillments, meanings"[17] for their adherents.

Third, very few studies actually consist of insights offered by Chinese Singaporeans who are Buddhists or Taoists that illuminate what has shaped and continues to shape their religious identity, and why they continue to adhere to these religions. As a result, current research has failed to incorporate the Buddhists' and Taoists' everyday experiences with spiritual realities enfolded within the religions. It is no wonder that Lai laments ". . . there continues to be a lack of in-depth knowledge, nuanced understanding . . . about various religions and the meanings of living in Singapore's multi-religious world."[18] This lack of knowledge and understanding could heighten potential misunderstanding and tensions, such as claims of ignorance and negative stereotyping, within Singapore's highly fragile multiracial and religious social fabric.

In light of this study's adoption of an expanded understanding of religious identity as a construct to examine why Chinese Singaporeans continue to adhere to Buddhism or Taoism, such an approach and the resulting insights can address a number of existing gaps within the broader studies of religious identity that have emerged largely from the West. These gaps, which will be further explicated in chapter 3, include the following key issues: (a) a truncated understanding of religious identity;[19] (b) a conflated use of religious identity with religious identification or religiosity;[20] (c) an

---

16. Goh, "Chinese Religion and the Challenge," 113.
17. Lai, "Conclusion," 692. See also Tong, *Rationalizing Religion*, 266.
18. Lai, "Introduction," xliii.
19. Bell, "Religious Identity," 3; Chen, "An Alternate View of Identity," 98. See also Browne et al., "Intercultural Inquiry of Religion," 3.
20. Dashefsky, "And the Search Goes On," 242; Hiroshi, "Documents Used in Rituals," 256; Tsomo, "Creating Religious Identity," 77; Ysseldyk et al., "Religiosity as Identity," 60.

overemphasis on the significance of external factors such as the various structures of society and social learning; and (d) minimizing, if not totally ignoring, the role of the divine or transcendent within religious identity—that the divine is "behind a broader natural description of religious identity formation and functioning."[21]

Rationale for Research

The discussion in the previous section reveals that current studies undertaken to explain the strength of Chinese Singaporeans' religious identity as Buddhists or Taoists have employed an imprecise use of religious identity and conflated it as part of social identity. Thus, these studies have largely highlighted societal structures as the primary dimensions that establish and sustain the adherents' religious identity. The other dimensions—such as the various forms of metaphysical realities—are largely ignored. Furthermore, these studies have also failed to incorporate the Buddhists' and Taoists' elucidation of their everyday experiences with spiritual realities enfolded within these religions.

In light of the broadened understanding of religious identity as defined in this study, which encompasses the key characteristics of the distinct but overlapping entities of religion and identity, the dimensions that establish and sustain the religious identity of Chinese Singaporeans who are either Buddhists or Taoists remain unclear.

Purpose of Research

The purpose of this grounded theory study is to discover and explain the dimensions that establish and sustain the religious identity of Chinese Singaporeans who are either Buddhists or Taoists. For this study, religious identity is defined as an individual's awareness of and commitment to: (a) a continuous and invigorating inner well-being, and (b) a sense of belonging and a need to extend the well-being to the sociocultural community associated with the divine. The awareness and commitment arise out of an individual's reciprocal interactions with the divine and the sociocultural community associated with the divine.

---

21. Bell, "Religious Identity," 5.

Introduction

In order to reach this goal, this study is guided by a central question: What are the dimensions that establish and sustain the religious identity of Chinese Singaporeans who are either Buddhists or Taoists? The sub-questions arising from this central question are:

1. How does ethnicity (i.e., being a Chinese) establish and sustain the religious identity of Chinese Singaporeans who are either Buddhists or Taoists?
2. How do family members or friends establish and sustain the religious identity of Chinese Singaporeans who are either Buddhists or Taoists?
3. How do Buddhist or Taoist associations, societies, or temples establish and sustain the religious identity of Chinese Singaporeans who are either Buddhists or Taoists?
4. How do Buddhist or Taoist teachings, rituals, and practices establish and sustain the religious identity of Chinese Singaporeans who are either Buddhists or Taoists?
5. How do family roles (e.g., son, daughter) and obligations establish and sustain the religious identity of Chinese Singaporeans who are either Buddhists or Taoists?
6. How does the transcendent—scriptures, bodhisattvas, gods, or deities—establish the religious identity of Chinese Singaporeans who are either Buddhists or Taoists?

Definition of Terms

1. *Chinese Singaporean.* In this study, Chinese Singaporean refers to a Chinese person who was born in Singapore, who attends or has attended state schools, and who predominantly uses English or Mandarin or a mix of English-Mandarin and other Chinese dialects to communicate with family members or friends.
2. *Race.* Official categories of race in Singapore refer to the classification assigned to the population.[22] There are currently four official categories or CMIO—Chinese (a person of Chinese origin such as Fujian, Cantonese, Hakka), Malay (a person of Malay or Indonesian origin),

---

22. Singapore Department of Statistics, *Census of Population 2010.*

Indian (of Indian, Pakistani, or Bangladeshi origin) and Others (all persons excluding Chinese, Malay, and Indian, such as Eurasians, Europeans, and Arabs).

3. *Religious identity.* Religious identity is defined as an individual's awareness of, and commitment to: (a) a continuous and invigorating inner well-being, and (b) a sense of belonging and a need to extend the well-being to the sociocultural community associated with the divine. This awareness and commitment arises out of an individual's reciprocal interactions with the divine and the sociocultural community associated with the divine. This broadened definition takes into account the overlapping key entities of religiosity or religion and identity, as discussed earlier.

4. *Dimensions.* In light of the unique and varied characteristics embedded within religious identity, this study will use *dimensions* in order to encapsulate and reflect the multiple and rich array of features or aspects that establish and sustain religious identity, which includes both the social as well as the transcendent.

5. *Buddhism* and *Taoism*. While these two religions, taken as a consolidated group, have the largest following in Singapore, they will be viewed as distinct Chinese religions. According to Tsomo, the traditional criterion to become a Buddhist is to "go for refuge in the Buddha, Dharma, and Sangha."[23] This criterion will be used in identifying the Buddhist participants. Furthermore, in Singapore local Buddhists and Taoists have recently undertaken efforts to differentiate themselves from each other.[24] For Buddhism, Clammer and Kuah-Pearce have detailed the extensive efforts primarily carried out by *reform Buddhism* or Reformist Buddhists[25] to eliminate the mythical elements from the religion that are associated with folk elements within Taoism/folk religion (see chapter 2 for the choice of this label). As for Taoism, this study has chosen to use the Wade-Giles form instead of the *Pinyin* form (i.e., Daoism). This is because the Wade-Giles form is the most common form used by Taoists in Singapore (e.g., Taoist

---

23. Tsomo, "Creating Religious Identity," 78.

24. Durai, "Buddhist Groups Reach Out"; Yen, "Taoists and Buddhists still Biggest Group."

25. Clammer, "Religious Pluralism and Chinese Beliefs," 203; Kuah-Pearce, *State, Society and Religious Engineering*, xi.

Federation and Taoist Youth) and in the official census reports released by the government. In 1990, the Taoist Federation was founded in Singapore to bring together various temples under an association. Later, in 2005, the federation initiated programs to educate the public on its faith and philosophy, with focus on the scriptures.[26] In the past, Chinese in Singapore have been practicing an amalgamated form of Buddhism, Taoism, and the prevailing folk beliefs and customs, which has been generically classified as "Shenism," Chinese religion, or Taoism/folk religion.[27]

Scope of Research

First, the key subjects of this study consisted of thirty-two Chinese Singaporeans—sixteen Buddhists and sixteen Taoists, both males and females. Since this research focused on Chinese who are born and raised in Singapore, the views of Chinese immigrants from surrounding countries (e.g., China, Malaysia, Taiwan) who are Buddhists or Taoists were not taken into account, even though many of them have become citizens of Singapore via immigration.

Second, the participants are current adherents of either Buddhism or Taoism and included both long-time and recent adherents. While there are no prescribed guidelines to determine what constitutes long-time or recent, the former consisted of those who have been adherents five years or more and the latter are those who have been adherents five years or less. Their previous religious backgrounds (i.e., those born into Buddhist or Taoist families or who have converted to Buddhism and Taoism) were not taken into consideration.

Third, in light of the growth of the number of Buddhists and Taoists among those who have received or are receiving higher education,[28] Buddhists and Taoists who are currently enrolled in institutions of higher education (e.g., university, polytechnic), or graduates from these institutions were also interviewed. Despite their exposure to more Western forms of education and thinking, uncovering the dimensions that cause them to

26. Yen, "Taoists and Buddhists still Biggest Group," para. 6.

27. Kuah-Pearce, *State, Society and Religious Engineering*, 21. See also Lee et al., *Taoism*, 147, and Tan, "Study of Chinese Religions," 140.

28. Choong, "Religious Composition of the Chinese," 334; Tan, "Keeping God in Place," 57.

turn to, or continue to adhere to, these traditional Chinese religions provided a richer understanding of the theory that emerged. At the same time, participants also included those who have not attended higher institutions of education. These participants have traditionally been viewed as associated with these religions. The data that was gleaned from interviewing these two groups of participants provided a more textured understanding of the resultant grounded theory.

Fourth, the interviewees included three groups—those introduced by Buddhist or Taoist temples or organizations, by friends or former colleagues, and those approached randomly in various Buddhist or Taoist temples or organizations. Interviewing a cross-section of different groups unveiled deeper and varied perspectives into the dimensions that undergird their religious identity as Buddhists or Taoists.

Finally, this study is designed to discover and describe the dimensions that shape the religious identity of Buddhists and Taoists in Singapore based on the accounts provided by the participants. It is not an attempt to validate the veracity of the spiritual or metaphysical constituents, despite the fact that these constituents have contributed significantly to the religious identity of the participants. Such an attempt calls for further research, which lies outside the scope of this study.

Limitations of Research

Due to the qualitative nature and limited focus of this study, the reasons for Chinese Singaporeans' adherence to Buddhism or Taoism do not explain why Buddhism and Taoism are expanding both in the rest of Asia and in the West.[29] Second, Chinese Buddhist and Taoist migrants from Malaysia, Hong Kong, Taiwan, and China to Singapore over the last two decades were not captured due to the scope of this study, even though they make up an important segment of the Chinese population in Singapore. Furthermore, this study did not capture the reasons why some Chinese Singaporeans choose to leave Buddhism and Taoism for other religions or atheism, despite efforts by these religions to renew themselves.

Third, the dimensions that establish and sustain the religious identities of Chinese Singaporeans who are either Buddhists or Taoists, emerging within the specific social context of Singapore, do not fully explain why

---

29. Jenkins, *The Next Christendom*, 217; Kohn and Roth; "Introduction," 8; Mitchell, *Buddhism*, 5–6.

Introduction

Buddhists or Taoists outside of Singapore choose to continue to practice their religions.

Fourth, the participants were not categorized according to the main schools of Buddhism and Taoism—i.e., Mahayana, Theravada, Vajrayana, 全真 (*Quan zhen*, or Complete Perfection) and 正一 (*Zhen yi*, or Orthodox Unity).

Fifth, as pointed out in the previous section, this study is not designed to validate the existence of spiritual realities.

Finally, this research did not account for those who continue to practice a syncretic mix of Buddhism, Taoism, and Chinese folk religions—i.e., Taoism/folk religion.

Significance of Research

A study into the dimensions that establish and sustain the religious identity of Chinese Singaporeans who are either Buddhists or Taoists is significant for three reasons. First, it will give the participants a voice in the current academic dialogues on religion and religious identity emerging from Singapore. This voice, which is elicited from the participants' experiences and perspectives, will also contribute to filling the existing void within the current studies of Buddhism and Taoism in Singapore as discussed earlier, and raise valuable questions and issues for future research.

Second, it is also the first qualitative study that explicitly draws upon an expanded understanding of religious identity, one that encompasses the critical facets from its separate entities as an analytical framework to discover and explain the dimensions that establish and sustain Singaporean Chinese individuals' religious identity as either Buddhists or Taoists from their point of view. This necessary approach[30] provides the possibilities to explore and discover dimensions beyond the current and widely accepted societal or environmental factors emphasized by studies that have emerged from Singapore. Thus, it can serve to generate richer insights that will fill the existing gaps within these studies.

Third, this study would furnish other religious communities within Singapore's dynamic religious landscape with richer resources to foster meaningful future interreligious interactions to sustain a peaceful religious climate in Singapore for the "larger interests of social cohesion, national

---

30. Chiew, "Chinese Singaporeans," 33–37.

unity and the common good."³¹ This is critical in light of the lack of nuanced understanding of the religions, the continued prominent role played by and transformations experienced by the religions, and the sensitivity of religious issues in Singapore.

Finally, this study has the potential to enrich and add to the increasing prominence of religious identity and how the larger body of Western-dominated identity research understands religious identity in the following ways. First, the study would provide non-Western perspectives on how religious identity is established and sustained through situating the context of study away from currently Western-dominated confines and into the world of Chinese Singaporeans who are Buddhists or Taoists. Such an approach would expand the current assumption that an individual is the center of the universe exerting autonomy and control³² over the establishing and maintaining of religious identity. Second, it would broaden the current limited understanding and undifferentiated use of religious identity with religious identification, both of which have arisen due to the subsuming of religious identity as part of social identity.³³

Lastly, it would raise awareness for future research on religious identity to be mindful of the active role of metaphysical realities and the abiding sense of well-being and rejuvenation as experienced by religious adherents. In light of the unique characteristics inherent within religious identity, research into the dimensions that establish and sustain it should not be reticent to investigate the contributions of the divine or transcendent realities and view any such attempts as "irrational and as therefore inherently problematic."³⁴

The next section examines and reviews key studies and theories that delineate the dimensions that establish and sustain religious identity—both emerging from Singapore and also the wider body of research in theories of identity. The review consists of two parts. In chapter 2, the focus is on the literature emerging from Singapore that seeks to account for the vitality of Buddhism and Taoism among the Chinese population. Subsequently, chapter 3 reviews theories that discuss how identity—religious or otherwise—is established and sustained.

---

31. Lai, "Conclusion," 691.
32. Chen, "An Alternate View of Identity," 99.
33. Hayward et al., "Recollections of Childhood Religious Identity," 80.
34. Hopkins, "Religion and Social Capital," 530.

Chapter 2

Review Of Studies On Buddhism And Taoism And Religious Identity In Singapore

In chapter 1, it was pointed out that numerous scholarly attempts have emerged from Singapore to account for the sustained vitality and prominence of practices and rituals associated with the ongoing revival of Buddhism and Taoism on the island. The previous chapter also highlighted that although these attempts are invaluable in producing insights into the developments of Buddhism and Taoism in Singapore, gaps remain in terms of how these studies define religious identity and the dimensions that establish and sustain it.

In light of the purpose of this study, the objectives of this chapter will be twofold. First, it will draw upon the relevant literature to serve as a backdrop for this study by examining the evolution of Buddhism and Taoism within the Chinese population and the current understanding of religious identity whenever the construct has been utilized, as well as the dimensions that establish and sustain it. Second, it will evaluate these attempts for the purpose of unveiling the contributions to this study and existing gaps.

The analysis of the available studies will be undertaken in three main sections. The first section will consist of studies that provide an overview of the Chinese population in Singapore and the impact of their dominant religions upon their identity—both prior to and after the island's independence. For the second section, the discussion of the studies investigating Buddhism and Taoism in Singapore will be guided by Chia's helpful categorization of existing studies of Buddhism in Singapore into general accounts, sociological studies, and historical studies.[1] Although his categorization has another section (i.e., country-specific studies) and he also examines studies that are micro in nature, these fall outside the parameters of this particular study.

According to Chia, general accounts of Buddhism in Singapore provide a general survey of Buddhist activities; sociological studies are attempts to theorize and analyze the characteristics and transformation of Buddhism in Singapore; and historical studies trace the development of Buddhism on the island over a broad period of time.[2] With available studies into Taoism's development in Singapore being less voluminous and at times done concurrently with Buddhism, this chapter groups these studies into the above-mentioned categories for ease of discussion and organization.

Within this section, space is also devoted to literature investigating the role of the Singaporean government in creating a "symmetrical identification"[3] between race and religious identification and practice. As Tong notes, "any analysis of religion in Singapore must deal with the role of the state ... the Singapore government has wielded significant influence on religious life in Singapore."[4] The final section will be a discussion of these studies, delineating how they have served to inform this study as well as the existing void that persists and how this study will be able to address them.

An Overview of Singapore's Chinese Community and Its Religious Practices

Pre-independence Period

Singapore is a small island with an area of less than three hundred square miles. While little is known of pre-colonial Singapore due to the fragmentary nature of existing records,[5] the arrival of Sir Stamford Raffles in 1819 and his securement of a treaty with the Temenggong of Johor transformed the island into a British trading post for the British East India Company and broke the Dutch dominance in the Straits of Malacca. The population

---

1. Chia, "Buddhism in Singapore," 81.
2. Ibid., 82–83.
3. Goh, "Christian Identities in Singapore," 2.
4. Tong, *Rationalizing Religion*, 2.
5. Turnbull, *History of Modern Singapore*, 19.

of the island then numbered about 1,000, consisting mainly of local *orang laut* (people of the seas), 120 Malays and about 30 Chinese.[6]

Upon gaining control of the island, the British adopted a free-port policy whereby no tariffs were imposed on goods traded on the island. Attracted by the opportunities to make large profits and more money, traders and immigrants flocked from China, India, and mainland Southeast Asia. As a result, both the island's trade and population expanded quickly. Among this growing and disparate population, the Chinese were the most populous. Between 1821 and 1901, the Chinese grew from about 20 percent of the population to over 70 percent.[7]

The arrival of the Chinese migrants from the southern regions of China also saw the import of their religious practices and traditions. During the colonial years, the Chinese community in Singapore remained "a cultural appendage of China,"[8] where it maintained a religious system that was both characteristically Chinese and influenced by changes in China, and also rearranged according to the circumstances of living in Singapore.[9]

Taoism/Folk Religion

Both Hu and C-B Tan point to two religions that have played critical roles throughout Chinese history.[10] The first, with no specific label, is known variously by scholars as *shenism,* 拜神 *bai shen* (i.e., "worship the gods"[11])

---

6. Chiew, "Chinese Singaporeans," 12.
7. Chiew, "Chinese in Singapore," 43. See also Lee, *British as Rulers*.
8. Freedman, *Study of Chinese Society*, 162.
9. Ibid., 168. See also Wang, *China and the Chinese Overseas*, 198.
10. Hu, "Religion and Philosophy in Chinese History," 82; Tan, "Study of Chinese Religions," 139.
11. Elliot, *Chinese Spirit-Medium Cults*, 27. See also Kuah-Pearce, *State, Society and Religious Engineering*, 21.

or 神教 *shen jiao* (i.e., "the doctrine of the gods"[12]), anonymous religion,[13] Siniticism,[14] religious Taoism/folk religion,[15] and Chinese religion.[16]

While these varied labels describe the same phenomenon, albeit with minor variations, an attempt to subscribe to a particular one will inevitably stir up ongoing debates concerning which label is more accurate in describing what early Chinese migrants believed and practiced. This is not the purpose of this research. However, in order to provide a focal term for consistency throughout the rest of the discussion, the label Taoism/folk religion will be adopted.

The adoption of the Taoism/folk religion label is based on (a) its close resemblance to the descriptions by a number of the Buddhist and Taoist participants in this research when they recounted what their parents or themselves practiced or are practicing, and (b) a recent publication on Taoism in Singapore by C. Y. Lee et al. under the auspices of the Taoist Federation (Singapore). The Taoist Federation was founded in 1990 with the support of local Taoist priests and devotees from *Quan zhen*, or Complete Perfection, and *Zhen yi*, or Orthodox Unity, the two dominant lineages of Taoism in Singapore. Lee notes that

> What passes for "Taoist" worship here ... shows more affinity with folk religion. The decisive difference in Singapore is that what may appear to be folk practices are in fact recognized officially as Taoist activities by the government. ... In the Singapore context the story of Taoism can hardly be understood apart from the popular religious traditions which have come to be cherished by the people and viewed officially as constitutive of the Taoist religion.[17]

Taoism/folk religion is the native religion of the Chinese civilization, as Hinduism is to India, dating back to time immemorial.[18] It is also highly complex, pluralistic, and syncretistic, amalgamating the traditions of Bud-

---

12. Wee, "'Buddhism' in Singapore," 170.

13. Topley, "Chinese Religion and Religious Institutions," 132–33. According to her, the popular religion of the Chinese people is marked by anonymity and lack of synthesis. She notes the difficulty of tracing all the historical processes that have resulted in the mass religious practices among the Chinese in Singapore.

14. Hu, "Religion and Philosophy in Chinese History," 82.

15. Lee et al., *Taoism*, 147.

16. C-B Tan, "The Study of Chinese Religions in Southeast Asia," 139, and Tong, "Religion," 370..

17. Lee et al., *Taoism*, 147-148.

18. Hu, "Religion and Philosophy in Chinese History," 82.

dhism, Confucianism, and the prevailing folk beliefs and customs such as ancestor worship and divination through the use of talismans, incantations, and rituals.[19]

Its complexity can be attributed to a number of key factors. First, according to Alan Elliot, the complexity is associated with the words of 拜 (*bai*, venerate, pray, or worship) and 神 (*shen*, or god).[20] In his view, the idea of worship has a number of connotations within the Chinese context. It can refer to physical actions associated with the performance of religious ceremonies (e.g., clasping of hands, burning of joss sticks) as well as mental attitudes (e.g., desire or intention to perform these ceremonies). As for *shen*, with no satisfactory equivalence in English—as *god* is inaccurate and laden with overtones of western theology and *spirit* is too impersonal—it is only possibly to define them as "powerful and spiritual beings . . . to be worshipped in order to secure human well being."[21]

Buddhism/Chinese Buddhism

The second religion is Buddhism, or more specifically Chinese Buddhism, which has developed and transformed since coming into contact with Chinese civilization in AD 65. Although Buddhism contributed various elements into the religious practices of the Chinese (for example Taoism adopted the practice of monasticism and produced the Taoist Canon following the form of Buddhist sutras), it was also influenced by the syncretism and polytheism of Taoism and Taoism/folk religion.[22] Thus, Chinese Buddhism entails the worshipping of Buddha and Boddhisattvas (e.g., *Guan yin pu sa*, 弥勒 *Mi le pu sa*, or Maitreya the Laughing Buddha), a mixture of Mahayana/Pure Land, Theravada, and Chan schools, and the incorporation of Buddhist and Taoist elements and images in the temples (e.g., magical or divination rites and Taoist deities placed in different rooms).

The long history of Buddhism in China and its close affinity with Taoism/folk religion has contributed to the blurring of boundaries between the two religions in the eyes of the Chinese settlers. Thus, Chinese Buddhism was naturally brought to Singapore as part of Taoism/folk religion.

---

19. Ibid., 84; Kuah-Pearce, *State, Society and Religious Engineering*, 54–57; Lee et al., *Taoism*, 161; Tan, "Study of Chinese Religions," 143–44.
20. Elliot, *Chinese Spirit-Medium Cults*, 27.
21. Ibid., 28.
22. See Ibid., 110, and Hu, "Religion and Philosophy in Chinese History," 82.

According to Vivienne Wee, a "significant number of the early migrants were already 'Buddhist' in one sense or another when they arrived."[23] Elliot also highlights that while many Chinese immigrants claimed to be Buddhists, the practice is highly likely to be *baishen*.[24] Thus, the religious system was marked by a lack of central theology and loss of pristine purity[25] with very little differentiation between, or devotion to, any particular tradition.[26]

While the Chinese migrants probably found it unnecessary to differentiate the complexities entailed in these religions, the religions played a pivotal role in the negotiation and construction of the early Chinese migrants' identity by fulfilling their functional, sociopsychological, and religious needs in an unfamiliar environment. Thus, each dialect group established its own temples—whether Buddhist or Taoist or an amalgamation of the two—as a "ritual foci"[27] within the area where each group congregated. In the view of C. Y. Lee et al., the number of temples increased significantly due to the rapid influx of Chinese immigrants.[28]

Post-independence Period

In June 1959, Singapore secured internal self-government from Britain and was granted "control over all domestic affairs, including finance."[29] The People's Action Party (PAP) became the island's first fully elected government. Under the leadership of Lee Kuan Yew, Singapore sought a merger with the newly independent Federation of Malaya in order to survive economically. Although the union was established in 1963, the widening divide over a host of issues (e.g., finance, taxation, race) brought an end to the tenuous relationship on August 8, 1965.

With independence thrust upon Singapore, the PAP-led government prepared to urgently address two immediate concerns—the development of economic viability and a sense of nationhood and solidarity. With the island being a settlement of immigrants, the government propounded that there were no indigenous tradition or shared myths that could be drawn

23. Wee, "'Buddhism' in Singapore," 158.
24. Elliot, *Chinese Spirit-Medium Cults*, 29.
25. Lau, "Buddhism and Youth in Singapore," 101.
26. Kuah-Pearce, *State, Society and Religious Engineering*, 22.
27. Freedman, *Study of Chinese Society*, 163.
28. Lee et al., *Taoism*, 152.
29. Turnbull, *History of Modern Singapore*, 268.

upon. Thus, Singaporeans were called to embrace a consumer-utilitarian culture and everything that stood in the way of economic development was removed under the guise of "creative destruction necessitated by capitalist development."[30] The legitimation of Singapore "was . . . from the very outset cast in economic rather than symbolic terms."[31]

Economic-dictated values became "the predominant defining characters of the high-growth city state,"[32] where competitiveness, meritocracy, and "an ethos of 'mutual trust and cooperation' between labor, employer and the state"[33] were inscribed upon the people. The workforce needed to be disciplined and the social environment made safe.[34] Furthermore, English, by virtue of it being a global and trade language, became the nation's working language and was officially adopted as the first language in all state schools in 1987.[35] At the same time, Singapore's commitment to secularism also ensured that racial and religious harmony was "jealously guarded by the state."[36]

The demographic composition of the Chinese community in post-independence Singapore resembles that of the 1900s, with the community comprising almost 77 percent of the population. However, while the label "Chinese" continues to refer to "a category or group of people of Chinese origin from the 19th century to the present in Singapore,"[37] much has changed in terms of culture (e.g., religion, language), social class position, and lifestyle.

John Clammer posits that since independence, the government's educational and cultural policies have weakened or eliminated the "old markers of Chinese identity, both within the . . . Chinese community and between the Chinese and other groups."[38] These markers include occupation, residence, religion, and language. Recognizing education and literacy in the English language as primary channels of upward mobility, many

---

30. Chua, "Foreword," ix.
31. Chua, "Racial-Singaporeans," 31. See also Kluver and Webber, "Patriotism and the Limits of Globalization," 386.
32. Chua, *Communitarian Ideology and Democracy*, 105.
33. Chua, "Racial-Singaporeans," 32.
34. Hong and Huang, *Scripting of a National History*, 1.
35. Turnbull, *History of Modern Singapore*, 317.
36. Tan, "Keeping God in Place," 55.
37. Chiew, "Chinese in Singapore," 65.
38. Clammer, "Chinese Ethnicity and Political Culture," 268.

Chinese Singaporeans pushed their children hard to excel in the mastery of English and other academic subjects.[39] The resulting high educational attainment ensured that the majority of the community prospered in tandem with the island's economic growth, demonstrated by the fact that its average monthly household income is the highest among all the ethnic groups.[40]

Despite the changes experienced by the Chinese community over the last four decades in the markers of its identity, Ah Eng Lai notes that its religious and cultural identification has remained stable and strong.[41] While there is an increasing propensity among the Chinese to convert to Christianity, Buddhism and Taoism as a consolidated group continue to be the dominant religions for the community. According to Eugene K. B. Tan, Robbie B. H. Goh, and the 2000 and 2010 censuses, Buddhism increased by a significant 15.5 percent between 1980 and 2000, and has continued to gain adherents over the last decade, especially among the higher-educated Chinese Singaporeans. Taoism, from 2000 to 2010, experienced a similar trend.[42]

Studies of Buddhism and Taoism in Singapore

General Accounts of Buddhism and Taoism

The earliest studies were mainly written in Chinese and focused on specific rituals or cults within Taoism/folk religion. For example in 1939, Han Wai Toon contributed an article on local Taoist deity—大伯公 (*Da bo gong*, or Grand Uncle) in a local Chinese newspaper. Other general accounts examined different Buddhist activities in Malaysia and Singapore, such as Colin McDougall's *Buddhism in Malaya*, written in the 1950s. Short articles, which also appeared sporadically in journals (e.g., *Ching Feng*) or magazines (e.g., *Buddhist Youth*) during the 1970s, dealt briefly with how Buddha Dharma could be used in Singapore, the state of Buddhism among youths, and Buddhism's apparent decline based upon responses to questionnaires given to pre-university and university students.[43]

39. Chiew, "Chinese Singaporeans," 15.
40. Tan, "Re-engaging Chinese-ness," 110.
41. Lai, "Introduction," xliii; Lai, "Conclusion," 690.
42. Tan, "Keeping God in Place," 57. See also Goh, "Christian Identities in Singapore," 3; Singapore Department of Census, *Census of Population 2000*, 34; Singapore Department of Census *Census of Population 2010*, 16.
43. Examples include Thera, "Buddha Dhamma and Singapore"; Lau, "Buddhism and Youth in Singapore"; and Tamney, "A Sociological Approach to Buddhism."

Review Of Studies On Buddhism And Taoism

Maurice Freedman's extensive anthropological research into the religious life of the Chinese community during the 1950s primarily examined the relationship between kinship and religion within the Chinese in Southeast Asia and Hong Kong.[44] His discussion on the Chinese society in Singapore centered on: (a) the role of associations, including secret societies, in providing solidarity and insulation for the immigrants, (b) the impact of marriage on kinship ties, especially among the Baba community, (c) the relationship between British colonial laws on family and customary Chinese laws, and (d) the religious rearrangement undertaken by the Chinese in light of the changes in China and local conditions.

His research also revealed how the local Chinese community adapted Buddhism and/or Taoism/folk religion. For example, he noted that while the various dialect groups were initially closely associated with the particular temples associated with the provinces or villages from whence they came, these immigrants gradually began to avail themselves of the services of the blossoming number of temples according to the "efficaciousness of their gods . . . or their (i.e., the gods') success in conferring special kinds of benefits."[45] At the same time, he briefly discusses the formation of three Buddhist organizations (i.e. Forest of Laymen, Singapore Federation of Buddhists, and Regional Center of the World Fellowship of Buddhists) that did not account for dialect groupings and also embraced members of other syncretic religions.

Marjorie Topley's observations of Buddhism in Singapore during the 1950s, also anthropological in nature, primarily focused on Chinese women's vegetarian houses and Chinese religion and its related religious institutions. The former refer to organizations formed by vegetarians with the purpose of "providing board and lodging for unattached women who worship Buddha."[46] These women were usually without family connections or abandoned by their husbands. Buddhism practiced by women in these houses was Pure Land, which is part of Mahayana Buddhism. It is characterized by the assimilation of many Taoist gods and goddesses and a belief in a paradise where all who recite *Amida* will be reborn into paradise upon death.

She also pointed out that Singapore then had a great variety of places besides temples that provided religious facilities and activities for the Chinese community. Particularly popular were the religious activities associated

---

44. Freedman, *Study of Chinese Society*.
45. Ibid., 166.
46. Topley, "Chinese Religion and Religious Institutions," 107.

with the temples. However, the adherents were not aware of the "borrowing and lending and even plagiarizing between Buddhism and Taoism."[47] Thus, religion was simply a "mass tradition handed down mainly by word of mouth . . . and of practices learnt in childhood by observation and imitation"[48] in order to be called upon when supernatural help was needed.

Another general account on Buddhism in Singapore is by Venerable Piyasilo or Piya Tan. In his *Buddhist Culture: An Observation of the Buddhist Situation in Malaysia and Singapore and a Suggestion*, he offers perspectives into "Buddhist national identity." Buddhist national identity is characterized as a cultural unity and spiritual ideal or commonness that serves to guide and unite all Buddhists in a particular nation.[49] As such, it is the culmination of the responses by the Buddhists in the nation to the Dharma according to the challenges that they encounter.

Liying Xu's recent article "Daoist Temples in Modern City Life: The Singapore City God Temple" examined the processes that a prominent Taoist temple underwent and how these resulted in the successful creation of a firm Taoist identity. The processes Xu examined included "historical background, approaches to management, and religious identity."[50] She noted that through the temple's transformation of leadership and management styles and choice of Taoism as its religious identity in tandem with the patterns of local and global social changes, it has "successfully established a Daoist identity."[51]

Sociological Studies on Buddhism and Taoism

A significant sociological study on Buddhism in post-independence Singapore is Vivienne Wee's "'Buddhism' in Singapore." She argues that, despite Buddhism's continued numerical dominance and use of a common label (*Buddhism*), the community does not share a "unitary religion."[52] In fact, there is a lack of correspondence and unity between the religious practices and beliefs of Buddhists in Singapore and what the Buddhist scriptures prescribed. Thus, she saw a need to differentiate between Buddhism and

47. Ibid., 133.
48. Ibid., 133.
49. Piyasilo, *Buddhist Culture*.
50. Xu, "Daoist Temples in Modern City Life," 115.
51. Ibid., 139.
52. Wee, "'Buddhism' in Singapore," 155.

Buddhism. The former refers to practices derived according to Buddhist canonical traditions—i.e., either Theravada or Mahayana. The latter, with no direct Buddhist canons, is the Singapore variety that demonstrates such a "range of beliefs, practices and institutions that it can be structured... into distinct and separate religious systems."[53] Although some of these systems, both in beliefs and practices, seem almost non- or nominally Buddhist, the adherents unequivocally declare themselves to be *Buddhists* and their religion *Buddhism*.

In view of these disparities, Wee argues that Singapore *Buddhism* must be viewed through a dialectical framework: it is both *Buddhism* as canonical Buddhism and *Buddhism* as Chinese syncretic religion, where the latter is a label for a "heterogeneous assemblage of religious systems."[54] While the majority of Singapore *Buddhists* are ignorant of these variations, she acknowledges that *Buddhism* in all its variety is fundamentally "a religious phenomenon primarily associated with the Chinese."[55]

Trevor Ling, a local sociologist, provided two articles in analyzing Buddhism in Singapore. The first is a paper entitled "Buddhism, Confucianism, and the Secular State in Singapore," where he examined the religious composition of Singapore in the 1980s, the nature of Singapore as a secular state, and the "degree of success which has been achieved in avoiding religiously generated ... social conflict."[56] Throughout the paper, he refers to Buddhists/Buddhism and Taoists/Taoism (alongside Christians, Muslims, Hindus) as religious identities, and demonstrates how the Buddhists and Taoists contributed to the "maintenance of peace and stability in Singapore"[57] vis-à-vis the religious policies adopted by the state.

His second contribution, which is a chapter in a book he edited, is entitled "Singapore: Buddhist Development in a Secular State." Using the Buddhist Triple Gems of the Buddha, Dharma, and Sangha as a framework, he traced the development of Buddhist temples, associations, and monks in Singapore. In observing the furnishings of the earlier temples in Singapore, he notes that they reflected an "already existing shared social identity."[58] He proposes that such prevailing solidarity enabled the communities then to

53. Ibid., 155.
54. Ibid., 180.
55. Ibid., 156.
56. Ling, "Buddhism, Confucianism, and the Secular State," 1.
57. Ibid., 17.
58. Ling, "Singapore," 155.

build and maintain these temples because such undertakings would have required considerable "practical and financial cooperation from a number of people."[59]

Over the last two decades, in the face of modernization, globalization, and loss of members to Christianity's aggressive proselytization, Buddhism and Taoism in Singapore have undergone significant changes. Various explanations have been put forth to account for these changes.

For Khun Eng Kuah-Pearce and Chee Kiong Tong, these religions have embarked on a process of rationalization or intellectualization in order to stay relevant to younger Singaporeans. This process includes an emphasis on the textual or doctrinal facets, abandonment of what are considered to be illogical or irrational beliefs, and intentional outreach that is akin to Christian practices (e.g., Dharma camps, handing out tracts, proselytization). While it is often assumed that these religions do not seek converts actively, the loss of their members to Christianity has spurred them towards active proselytization.[60] These efforts are apparently paying off due to the continuous growth in the number of Buddhists and Taoists, especially among those who have been, or are, pursuing higher education.

In Kuah-Pearce's extensive exploration of the rise of Reformist Buddhism in Singapore, which was also highlighted by Clammer[61] albeit using a slightly different label (reform Buddhism), she argues that the rationalization and bureaucratization processes, which began in the 1970s, reflect the confluence of three key factors: a) the active intervention of the PAP-led government, b) disenchantment of the younger Chinese Singaporeans towards existing practices within Chinese religion, Buddhism and Taoism, and c) the aggressiveness of the Christian community in evangelism. Thus, as these factors interacted with one another, they set in motion the need to remove the "mythical and supernatural elements from both the Buddhist and Shenist (or Taoism/folk religion) practices."[62]

According to her, Reformist Buddhism is characterized by a number of features. The first is an emphasis on scriptural tenets that include the Four Noble Truths, the theory of *karma*, rebirth and merit-making,

---

59. Ibid., 155.

60. Tong, *Rationalizing Religion*, 130.

61. Clammer, "Religious Pluralism and Chinese Beliefs," 203–4.

62. Kuah-Pearce, *State, Society and Religious Engineering*, 9. See also Kuah-Pearce's work, which is also cited by Chia's tracing of the development of The Buddhist College of Singapore. See Chia, "Teaching Dharma, Grooming Sangha."

Buddhist work ethics, and the Eightfold Path. Second, its organization is decentralized, with lay Buddhist groups carrying out various activities with the monks as participants. Worship and activities are held in residential or office buildings instead of religious buildings or temples. Kuah-Pearce points out that the utilization of lay groups and refocusing on doctrinal Buddhism have "changed the religious practices and landscape of the Chinese,"[63] with many younger Chinese Singaporeans being active participants in Reformist Buddhist activities.

Third, the key activities of the Reformist Buddhists fall into two main categories—religious and secular. The former includes spreading Buddhist knowledge to the public, nurturing a group of committed Reformist Buddhists, performing missionary work, and subtle proselytization. The latter includes cultural, civic, educational, and welfare activities, such as supporting government campaigns (e.g., respecting your elders, using Mandarin instead of dialects) that are in line with Buddhism, and setting up welfare homes for the aged and organizing cultural tours to Buddhist and non-Buddhist countries.

As a result of these efforts, she surmises that Reformist Buddhism has emerged as a force to challenge "Christianity's claims to modernity."[64] She points out that in Singapore, a person's religious identity is closely associated with class identity. Thus, Christianity's historical and continued association with the West, as well as the majority of Christians comprising society's middle and upper classes, have resulted in the religion being viewed "as a high class religion."[65]

Another comprehensive attempt is Chee Kiong Tong's study of Chinese religions in Singapore. Through a historical perspective, as well as drawing from quantitative data to track the trends and changes in the face of modernization, he seeks to address the current shortcomings in the current literature, the gaps between "the nature and boundaries of Chinese religion and the relationship between folk and canonical religions,"[66] and the religious shifts that are ongoing in Singapore (e.g., intellectualization, conversion).

Tong asserts that there is a process of intellectualization or rationalization of Buddhism and Taoism in Singapore, arguing that this process

---

63. Kuah-Pearce, *State, Society and Religious Engineering*, 232.
64. Ibid., 286.
65. Ibid., 271.
66. Tong, *Rationalizing Religion*, 31.

reflects "one of the main features of a modern society [that] is the process of rationalization"[67]—where humans undergo a process of clarifying, specifying, and systematizing the reasons for their existence. Religion, being an integral part of every human, is similarly subjected to the same process. Tong notes that rationalization does not mean the decline of the significance of religion, but rather that changes occur in the nature and role of religion.

A key facet within the intellectualization or rationalization of Buddhism and Taoism in Singapore is the demystification of religious beliefs and practices. Demystification is characterized by two key actions. The first is the discarding by Buddhists and Taoists of what they "perceive to be the irrationalities of the religions, and attempt to locate what they consider to be orthodox beliefs."[68] Thus, there is a search for a textual religion rather than merely following traditional practices. The second is the doctrinal and structural reorganization of Buddhist and Taoist federations and associations in order to systematically present the teachings of Buddhism and Taoism to young Singaporeans. As such, tracts are published, public talks or rallies are held, and camps are organized in order to enlarge membership.

At the same time, Tong attributes the rationalization process to religious competition in an environment where major world religions (e.g., Buddhism, Christianity, Islam) and a host of minor religions (e.g., Soka Gakkai, Sathya Sai Baba) coexist in such close proximity. With the threat of losing followers to other religions, especially in light of Christianity's perceived aggressiveness, Buddhists and Taoists have no choice but to be proselytizing religions. At the same time, these religions have also increasingly differentiated themselves in order to help young Singaporeans gain a clearer picture of each religion's beliefs and rituals.

The rationalization theme is continued in Vineeta Sinha's analysis of how Taoism and Hinduism in Singapore have points of convergence by tracing (a) the complexities and ambiguities that undergird the current discussions of these two religious options which Singaporeans commonly use "to signal their religious identities,"[69] and (b) the organizational transformations these two religions undertook in the face of pressures to modernize and arrest the rate of decline in number of adherents between the 1990s and 2000.

According to Sinha, with the ties between ethnic identities and specific religions "no longer deemed to be absolutely binding, with the strong

---

67. Ibid., 5.
68. Ibid., 5.
69. Sinha, "'Hinduism' and 'Taoism' in Singapore," 123.

possibility of religious conversion as well as the rejection of religious identity altogether,"[70] the aim of Taoism's reforms is to appeal to the English-speaking Chinese Singaporeans through deprioritizing the ritualistic and superstitious elements and highlighting the philosophical or theological elements (e.g., the *Dao de jing*). While Sinha notes that such a move has brought about tensions within Taoism, particularly between the leaders who focus either on the philosophical or folk versions, it is apparent that the approach is working in light of the increase in Taoist adherents among those who have received higher education.

According to Daniel P. S. Goh, the key to understanding the changes within Chinese religion is to

> . . . conceptualize the relationship between syncretism and the two processes of change captured by the *transfiguration* of forms brought about by mediation in new or accelerating cultural-economic flows and the *hybridization* of meanings brought about by contact between different cultural systems.[71]

His approach does not see modernity as a superior system that forces Chinese religion to play catch-up or rationalize by appropriating modern Western religion (i.e., Christianity). Instead, the dynamism inherent in the syncretic nature of Chinese religion that caused it to successfully assimilate various practices (rational or otherwise) for over a thousand years allows it to reinvent itself as a response to the intrusion of modernity.

He defines transfiguration as "the changing of forms of practices without the shift in essential meanings" and hybridization as "the change in meaning with little change to forms of religious practice."[72] An example of the former is the shift undertaken by a 77-year old Taoist temple, which used to be dedicated to the worship of a local Malay *shen* or god (Datuk Gong), to incorporate two other gods (*Da bo gong* and *Ganesha*) to represent the Chinese, Malay, and Indian populations in line with the government's emphasis on multiracialism. The latter is demonstrated by the Reform Taoists' recent attempts to highlight canonical Taoism as the "unifying center of Chinese religion without excluding the popular aspects."[73]

Eugene K. B. Tan's "Keeping God in Place: The Management of Religion in Singapore" is an attempt to explore how a strong religious identity

70. Ibid., 147.
71. Goh, "Chinese Religion and the Challenge," 110.
72. Ibid., 113.
73. Ibid., 128.

coexists with a strong Singaporean identity. Drawing from the impact of global religious resurgence and fundamentalism upon Singapore's fragile multireligious landscape, and the government's institutional and legal framework (e.g., Penal Code and Sedition Act, Internal Security Act, and the Maintenance of Religious Harmony Act) to check these external influences and manage religious harmony, he argues that the present racial and religious stability and civility on the island does not mean the absence of underlying religious competition and "occasional distrust and misunderstanding between religious groups."[74]

With each religion answering to a higher truth and simultaneously a core part of Singaporeans' identities, these tensions surface occasionally. Thus, in order to take religions seriously and yet maintain cordial interreligious relations, Eugene K. B. Tan calls for "the necessity and appreciation by the state, policymakers, society, and faith communities in understanding the subtleties and complexities in which religion and public life impact each other."[75]

Other sociological and political discourses of how national or religious identity is established and sustained in Singapore have largely focused on the active role of the state. The state or government must not be neglected as it "is present in most areas of everyday life. It attempts to manage, through social policies, every aspect of social life."[76] Clammer notes that, with Singapore emerging as a new state in 1965, the problem of identity has been so paramount that there is an ongoing search to "find images around which an allegedly common identity can be constructed."[77] Eventually, what emerged as the Singaporean identity has been shaped primarily by the government's subscription to the "culture of capitalism."[78]

For Tan, as noted earlier, the Singapore government plays an active role in ensuring that a strong religious identity (i.e., being a Buddhist, Muslim, or Taoist) coexists with a strong Singaporean identity. He points out that the government is acutely aware that "religious differences tend to reinforce racial and culture identities and differences."[79] For example, amongst the Malays, racial and religious identities—i.e., Malay-Muslim—are both

74. Tan, "Keeping God in Place," 76.
75. Ibid., 76.
76. Tong, *Rationalizing Religion*, 2.
77. Clammer, "Chinese Ethnicity and Political Culture," 203.
78. Chua, "Racial-Singaporeans," 32.
79. Tan, "Keeping God in Place," 58.

prominent and conflated. Thus, the government takes preemptive actions, particularly through key legislations, to keep strong religious identities or identifications in check and mobilize them for the purposes of building a Singaporean identity.

In Robbie B. H. Goh's analysis, Singapore's multicultural policy adopted by the government has resulted in race being simplified into the official categories of Chinese, Malay, Indian, and Others (CMIO). Besides a constant pressure to align one's racial identity with official racial distinctions, the policy reinforces the pegging of racial identification with cultural and religious practices. Thus, to be Chinese is to speak Mandarin even though there are many distinct dialects being used by different dialect groups (e.g., Cantonese, Hakka, Fujian).[80]

At the same time, the Mandarin-speaking segment of the Chinese population is identified officially (e.g., Singapore Department of Statistics, 2000) as adherents of traditional Chinese religions (e.g., Buddhism, Taoism). Goh notes that this connection between religion and cultural-racial identity is the "effect of a type of self-perpetuating institutional narrative and taxonomy."[81] Against this backdrop, he also points out that the Christian identity in Singapore occupies "a distinctive and often uncomfortable position."[82]

Other studies have also highlighted the close alignment between official race categories and religious affinity, primarily due to the nation's multicultural policy.[83] In Kuah-Pearce's opinion, the state sees "each ethnic group as closely affiliated to one religion."[84] In the *Census of Population 2000*, it notes that the majority of the Chinese who speak mainly Mandarin or Chinese dialects accordingly practice the traditional Chinese religions of Buddhism, Taoism, or traditional Chinese religion of ancestor worship.[85]

---

80. Goh, "Christian Identities in Singapore," 2.

81. Ibid., 3.

82. Ibid., 7.

83. Kuah-Pearce, *State, Society and Religious Engineering*, 4–6; Tong, *Rationalizing Religion*, 49.

84. Kuah-Pearce, *State, Society and Religious Engineering*, 5.

85. Singapore Department of Statistics, *Census of Population 2000*.

Historical Studies on Buddhism and Taoism

One of the most recent historical studies on Buddhism in Singapore is Y. D. Ong's *Buddhism in Singapore—A Short Narrative History*, in which he traces the main development of "the three main Buddhist traditions—Chinese Mahayana, Theravada and Vajrayana (Tibetan Buddhism) in Singapore and the current state of Buddhism in this island state."[86] In one section, Ong focuses on the "immediate post-war effort to foster a Buddhist identity through lay organizations, founding of schools, the formation of the Singapore Buddhist Federation and the petition to have Vesak Day declared as a public holiday."[87] Towards the end of the section, he notes that despite the progress made, much remained to be done for a "clear Buddhist identity . . . to be forged"[88]—especially in terms of educating the local populace in Buddhism and the correct Buddhist practices.

Guan Thye Hue's dissertation 中华传统宗教信仰在东南亚的蜕变：新加坡的道教和佛教研究 (*Zhong hua chuan tong zong jiao xin yang zai tong nan ya de tui bian: Xin jia po de dao jiao he fo jiao yan jiu*—The Transformation of Traditional Chinese Religious Beliefs in South-east Asian Society: A Case Study of Taoism and Buddhism in Singapore), details the development of these two religions beginning with their arrival with the earliest Chinese immigrants to the present day. Through both historical and sociological analysis, it examines changes in their religious activities and a variety of forces that have shaped these two religions in Singapore.[89]

Hue notes that a primary motivation for Taoism's growth in Singapore is to be found in 善 (*shan*, or good)—i.e. engaging in good works such as generously donating to charitable organizations and building schools. In terms of Taoism's unity, it is undergirded by 乩 (*ji*, or shaman). Although shamans belong properly to Chinese folk religion and were prominent prior to Singapore's rapid development, their existence today in many of the Taoist temples in Singapore has become a unifying force—drawing Taoists together in attempts to delineate their future role such that the religion will continue to be uniquely Singaporean in its characteristics and at the same time not be labeled by the younger generation as superstitious and backward.

---

86. Ong, *Buddhism in Singapore*, 12.
87. Ibid., 12.
88. Ibid., 84.
89. Hue, "Zhong hua chuan tong zong," ii.

As for Buddhism in Singapore, Hue observes the religion as exemplified by 宽容 (*kuan rong*, or broadmindedness). Three examples were given to support his observations: (a) the harmonious coexistence of the different forms of Buddhism that originated from various countries (e.g. Japan, Sri Lanka, Thailand, China, and Taiwan), (b) the initiatives undertaken by the Buddhists to reach out and demonstrate respect to other major religions on the island for the purpose of strengthening mutual trust and religious harmony, and (c) the recent collaborations with other charities established by the Hindus and Muslims to serve the impoverished. As a result, he notes that Buddhism in Singapore has evolved and embodies the multiracial characteristic of the island.

In order to foster a deeper understanding of Taoism for adherents and nonadherents in Singapore, C. Y. Lee et al. co-wrote *Taoism: Outlines of a Chinese Religious Tradition*. The book provides an overview of the key facets of Taoism—historical development, Taoist ritual, and Taoism in Singapore. According to them, Taoist presence on the island could be as early as the 15th century, when the famous Chinese maritime explorer Admiral 郑和 (*Zheng he*) visited Southeast Asia and introduced the worship of 天后 (*Tian hou*) or 妈祖 (*Ma zu*), also known as the Empress of Heaven. To date, *Tian hou* continues to be one of the two most popular Taoist deities in Singapore, the other being *Da bo gong*.

In Lee's analysis, a distinctive feature of Taoism in early Singapore is factionalism—primarily over which dialect group the adherents belong to, such as 福建 (Fujian), 潮州 (Chaozhou), or 广东 (Guangdong), and the Taoist temples built by each group. The existence of factionalism demonstrates "the intimate relationship between popular Taoist worship and dialect affiliation."[90] However with the government's all-out efforts to promote the use of Mandarin among Chinese Singaporeans since the 1980s, factionalism of this nature is waning and instead has been replaced by tensions between the leaders of folk Taoism and philosophical Taoism over the future of Taoism in Singapore. In moving forward, the Taoist Federation will need to negotiate these tensions so as to move Taoism beyond the current concerns of folk rituals.

---

90. Lee et al., *Taoism*, 152.

Discussion

Singapore continues to be a profoundly religious society amidst the rapid pace of modernization. Religious identification continues to be strong, so much so that "religious faith is a major part of Singapore's cultural ballast."[91] For the Singaporean Chinese, the majority are Buddhists or Taoists. Existing studies on these two religions, of which quite a number have been examined in this chapter, undoubtedly provide rich insights into the developments that these two religions have undergone in Singapore in the face of rapid industrialization in order to meet the needs of the adherents. However, three key gaps emerge, especially in light of this study's purpose to discover and explain the dimensions that undergird the religious identity of Chinese Singaporeans either as Buddhists or Taoists.

First, where the term "religious identity" has been used in the existing studies discussed above, it has succumbed to the concept's popular but undifferentiated use[92] within the wider literature as discussed in the previous chapter. Thus, it remains largely undefined, imprecise, and is often assumed to be a group category or social/religious label as part of social identity, for example in the works of Robbie Goh, Kuah-Pearce, Ling, Sinha, Charlene Tan, Eugene Tan, and Xu. At the same time, it has also been used in an undifferentiated manner alongside religious identification or the active process of being associated with either of the religions.

As a result of this oversimplification and undifferentiated use of the term, these studies have failed to examine how the characteristics associated with two entities that undergird the notion of religious identity—i.e., religion and identity—serve to provide inspiration and motivation for the Buddhists and Taoists to continue to adhere to their respective religions. Furthermore, no attempts have been undertaken to discover and explain the adherents' insights in terms of the dimensions that establish and sustain their religious identity.

Second, the studies have remained mainly ethnographical, historical, sociological, or anthropological observations, and they have examined the religions "in an overarching and extensive manner rather than looking at specific issues... of... practices, organizations, personalities, and so on."[93] The research by Ong, Hue, and Lee et al. (see above) are primarily general

---

91. Singapore Government, *Shared Values*, 8.
92. Brubaker and Cooper, "Beyond 'Identity,'" 2.
93. Chia, "Buddhism in Singapore," 81.

surveys over an extensive time period, where the developmental cycles of the two religions are painted in broad strokes, providing an overview of the key milestones and personalities that have impacted the religions. While Xu's work is less extensive in scope and focused on a particular temple, her study is preoccupied with how the temple has adapted itself in light of Singapore's rapid modernization and its subsequent ability to play a leading role among Taoists in Singapore today.

Similarly Marjorie Topley's and Maurice Freedman's works, while providing readers with empirical observations of the religious practices and institutions (e.g., temples, monasteries, vegetarian houses) among the Chinese in early Singapore, are primarily ethnographic surveys. Their focus is also largely limited to certain segments of the Chinese community (e.g., Cantonese women, vegetarian halls 斋堂 zhaitang), instead of extending their sample group to include other segments.[94] As these studies are primarily surveys, there is a limited analysis of the religions practiced by the Chinese. For example, both Topley and Freedman devoted only small sections within their works to briefly examine the characteristics of how traditional Chinese religions were adapted by Chinese immigrants in light of the sociocultural conditions of the island.

As for Wee's assessment of *Buddhism* in Singapore, she sought to demonstrate its disparities with canonical Buddhism by providing an historical overview of how the former was intertwined with elements of Chinese syncretic religions and the characteristics of the latter when it first arrived, and how it has developed in Singapore. While her review of the state of *Buddhism* in Singapore is accurate in pointing out the local version is a label for an "apparently heterogeneous assemblage of religious systems,"[95] it remains general and anecdotal in nature and her conclusions about the majority of Singapore's *Buddhists* being ignorant of Buddhist philosophy and differences between the various schools have not taken the views of local *Buddhists* into account.

Third, the dominant consensus of these studies is that external factors, such as structural renewals undertaken by Buddhism and Taoism, the important role of religious leaders and the Singapore government, and ethnicity, largely account for the continued vibrancy of these religions among Chinese Singaporeans today. For example, Kuah-Pearce's account of the rise of Reformist Buddhism in Singapore, which remains one of the most

---

94. See also DeBernardi, "Introduction," 4–5.
95. Wee, "'Buddhishm' in Singapore," 180.

extensive in terms of her attempt to trace the transformation of Chinese religion in the face of modernization, points to the process of *Buddhicisation* of Chinese religious syncretism, and the active role of the government, Sangha, and Reformist Buddhists within the Chinese community.

As for Tong, part of his extensive study into religious shifts includes "probably the first quantitative study of Chinese ritual practices . . . for the analysis of religious changes in Chinese religions."[96] He notes that such a survey is important because religious participation is "an important indicator of religious commitment."[97] While his study provides rich insights into the shifts that have occurred in the practices (e.g. worship activities, birth, or death rituals) undertaken and the environmental conditions that the shifts are predicated upon (e.g. education level, ethnicity, gender, dialect groups), it does not explore other dimensions that provide the motivation for religious participation and commitment. Similarly, in the studies by Robbie Goh, Hue, Sinha, and Charlene Tan, the exploration of structural changes also predominate—whether these have taken place within the religions due to the efforts of the religions' leaders or arisen from the role of the Singapore government in initiating these changes.

These observations by the researchers have provided a foundational understanding of how Buddhism and Taoism have evolved and transformed in Singapore amidst the changing nature of the country and the needs of the adherents. However, the overemphasis on external factors also means that the studies fail to account for the views of the adherents, particularly in terms of what the latter views as the dimensions that undergird their continued adherence to these religions. In light of religious identity constituting the entities of religion (i.e., originating from, and answering to, a higher truth as well as affirmation of various metaphysical constituents) and identity (i.e., awareness and commitment to inner well-being, a sense of belonging, and need to extend well-being), then surely there are valuable insights to be gleaned through utilizing it as an analytical construct to discover and explain the dimensions that sustain the religious identity of Singaporean Chinese who are either Buddhists or Taoists.

In order to use religious identity as a research construct, this study began by proposing that the definition of the concept needs to be broadened to encompass the critical characteristics associated with the distinct entities of identity and religion. Drawing upon this broadened definition as the

---

96. Tong, *Rationalizing Religion*, 195.
97. Ibid., 157.

foundation, the next step was to create a series of interview questions (see Appendix A) that provided opportunities for the adherents to articulate the dimensions that they perceive to be undergirding their religious identity as adherents of Buddhism or Taoism. The interview process and questions will be further discussed in chapter 4.

By situating the research in the world of the adherents—being sensitive to the realities of their experiences and listening to their internal narratives—this study strives to derive a more robust understanding of religious identity and the dimensions that undergird it. As noted in chapter 1, this understanding has the potential to provide insights to address the gaps existing within larger body of studies into theories of identity, religious or otherwise. In the next chapter, attention will be given to examining these theories of identity.

CHAPTER 3

REVIEW OF THEORIES OF IDENTITY AND RELIGIOUS IDENTITY

IN THE PREVIOUS CHAPTER, attempts have been made to examine the relevant studies emerging from Singapore that have sought to explain the unabated vitality of Buddhism and Taoism on the island. The chapter sought to point out how these studies inform our understanding of religious identity and the dimensions that establish and sustain it for Chinese Singaporeans who are either Buddhists or Taoists. Yet, it is also critical to note that attempts to understand religious identity and the dimensions that undergird it must be framed within the wider body of theories of identity, especially in light of how the latter has significantly influenced the development of the notion of identity and the facets related to the notion.

Thus, the purpose of this chapter is twofold. First, it seeks to explore pertinent studies that explore processes or dimensions responsible for establishing and sustaining the development of identity (particularly religious identity) such that it becomes a salient base for self-conception and conduct.[1] Second, it will consider the contributions and existing gaps of these studies, and delineate the potential of this study to address these gaps.

This chapter consists of three sections. The first section entails an overview of the historical development of the theories of identity. Particular attention will be given to the process Philip Gleason labels as "the emergence and diffusion of identity."[2] This process is characterized by the

---

1. See for example Ashmore and Jussim, "Introduction"; Bell, "Religious Identity"; Cote and Levine, *Identity Formation, Agency and Culture*.

2. Abrams, "Social Identity, Social Cognition," 201; Hogg et al., "Tale of Two Theories," 255.

gradual departure of identity from its original meaning, that of continuity or sameness, into one that is ambiguous, constructed, multiple, and fluid.[3] As a result of diffusion, the concept has become so ambiguous that it is undifferentiated from terms like "religious identification" and "religiosity."

In light of this attempt, this section will survey theories developed within two broad phases of development—early and latter development. The former phase entails Erik Erikson's psychosocial conceptualization of identity and James E. Marcia's empirical model consisting of four statuses (i.e., diffusion, foreclosure, moratorium, and achieved), which claims to be able to explain how young people engage in identity formation.[4] The latter phase reviews the two main perspectives represented in subsequent research of the concept—identity theory in sociology and social identity theory in psychology.

The second section specifically examines the literature that has drawn upon and extended the theoretical foundations of Erikson, Marcia, social identity theory, and identity theory in examining how religious identity is established and sustained, or how religion serves as a salient source to promote the forging and contouring of identity.[5] These studies generally assume identity to be nonexistent apart from external influences such as social and developmental processes, and religions as a basis for social and personal identity. Thus, religious identity is by necessity conceptualized and used interchangeably as a social or group category and assumed to be a continually evolving process of *becoming* rather than *being* due to social changes and culture and ethnic backgrounds.[6]

The final section consists of a discussion of the reviewed literature, delineating how these have served to provide useful constructs in understanding the nature of identity—religious or otherwise—and the dimensions that establish and sustain it. At the same time, as in the previous chapter, this section will also reveal the existing gaps within these studies and address how the insights that emerge from this study have the potential to address these gaps.

---

3. Gleason, "Identifying Identity," 911.

4. Ibid., 911. Also Kohn and Roth, "Introduction," 1–3, and Brubaker and Cooper, "Beyond 'Identity,'" 3.

5. Kroger, "Ego Identity Status Research," 145.

6. King, "Religion and Identity," 197; Peek, "Becoming Muslim," 218.

An Overview of Theories of Identity and Identity Formation

Early Development

Semantically, *identity* is derived from the Latin root *idem*, which indicates sameness and lack of change or deviation.[7] It has been in use in English since the sixteenth century, initially by rational thinkers such as Locke, Kant, and Kierkegaard as a "function of consciousness, a personal sense of reflection and self-awareness created actively by the thinking, rational ego."[8] For Johannes Van der Ven, drawing from another Latin term *identitas*, identity refers to a "way in which the *substantia* of an entity remains the same despite all the changes undergone by its *accidents*."[9] In other words, at the fundamental level, identity encapsulates an individual's awareness of a continuity of an inherent solidity regardless of the transformations he or she has undergone.

Erik Erikson

Within the social sciences, the term *identity* did not appear as any analytical concept before the early 1940s. By the 1980s, it became a common technical term.[10] The dominance of the term can be attributed to the foundational work of Erik Erikson—"the 'father of the identity concept,'"[11] who used identity as the central concept undergirding human development, historical change, and personal well-being.

In *Identity and the Life Cycle*, Erikson first advanced the key concept of ego identity—i.e., the "accrued confidence that one's ability to maintain inner sameness and continuity ... is matched by the sameness and continuity of one's meaning for others."[12] Explicating it later, Erikson points out that ego identity "concerns more than a mere fact of existence; it is ... the

---

7. Hopkins, "Religion and Social Capital," 530; Kohn and Roth, "Introduction," 3, 7.
8. Gleason, "Identifying Identity," 911–12.
9. Kohn and Roth, "Introduction," 1.
10. Van Der Ven, "The Communicative Identity," 24.
11. Weigert et al., *Society and Identity*, 5.
12. Cote and Levine, *Identity Formation, Agency and Culture*, xiii. See also Weigert et al., *Society and Identity*, 6–8.

ego quality of this existence."[13] Thus, it is an inherent sense or awareness of this invigorating sameness and continuity, which Erikson also labels as an "optimal sense of identity or sense of psychosocial well-being."[14] While it is primarily characterized by a "feeling of being at home in one's body ... sense of 'knowing where one is going,'"[15] there is also an inner assuredness of recognition from those who count.

The formation of this "optimal sense of identity"[16]—which is characterized by psychosocial well-being, accrued confidence, and invigorating continuity—occurs over time when an individual successfully negotiates a cumulative series of identifications. Identifications consist of a "selective repudiation and mutual assimilation of childhood identifications . . . dependent on the process by which a society . . . identifies the young individual."[17] In the event an individual is unsuccessful in his or her attempts to integrate, whereby an individual experiences a gap between his or her childhood identity and the incomplete formation of a new identity, despair or identity crisis will emerge.

In order to overcome this despair or restoration, Erikson surprisingly points to the role of religion. In *Identity: Youth and Crisis*, he states that religion "restores, at regular intervals and through rituals significantly connected with the important crises . . . a new sense of wholeness, of things rebound."[18] The restoration comes about through an individual's faith or a demonstration of his or her smallness and dependence through humility, akin to a "childlike surrender to a Provider or providers who dispense earthly fortune as well as spiritual health."[19]

As the term "identity" grew increasingly popular and became diffused after Erikson first used the term, he sought to review the concept and provide a "delimitation of what [it] is and what it is not."[20] He admits that the concept of identity is so difficult to grasp because of its elusive nature—a "process 'located' in the core of the individual and yet also in the core of his

---

13. Erikson, *Identity and the Life Cycle*, 94.
14. Erikson, *Identity*, 50.
15. Erikson, *Identity and the Life Cycle*, 128.
16. Erikson, *Identity*, 163.
17. Erikson, *Identity and the Life Cycle*, 122.
18. Erikson, *Identity*, 83.
19. Ibid., 67.
20. Ibid., 15.

communal culture."[21] Thus, he asserts that any discussion of identity formation cannot dichotomize the simultaneous processes of reflection and observation, where individuals evaluate themselves in light of how they perceive others to be evaluating them.

In other words, the formation of the personal code or referent system occurs when individuals synthesize their concerns about "what they appear to be in the eyes of others as compared to what they feel inside."[22] In Livia Kohn and Harold Roth's opinion, this introduction of others into the investigation of identity marked "a first foray into defining identity not merely on the basis of the individual but also the function of social groups and larger communities."[23]

James E. Marcia

While Erikson provided insightful descriptions into the nature and process of identity formation, Marcia's development of the Ego Identity Status Paradigm highlights "the possibility of qualitatively different styles . . . in the identity formation process."[24] Marcia's model seeks to move away from the overgeneralized polar outcomes of ego/optimal identity and negative identity/identity crisis through developing measures and criteria to assess the degree of ego identity. Thus, while Erikson's identity achievement and identity diffusion serve as starting points, albeit on opposite ends, Marcia argues for "two additional concentration points roughly intermediate in this distribution"[25]—i.e., moratorium and foreclosure.

He defines an identity-achievement person as one who has "experienced a crisis period and is committed to an occupation and ideology."[26] On the other hand, an identity diffusion person may or may not have experienced a crisis and is characterized by a lack of commitment. In terms of ideological matters, he or she is either uninterested or "takes a smorgasbord approach in which one outlook seems as good . . . as another and . . . is not adverse to sampling from all."[27]

21. Ibid., 22.
22. Ibid., 261.
23. Kohn and Roth, "Introduction," 2.
24. Kroger, "Ego Identity Status Research," 145.
25. Marcia, "Development and Validation," 552.
26. Ibid., 551.
27. Ibid., 552.

An individual who is in moratorium is undergoing a crisis as he or she struggles to form commitments. Thus, these commitments remain largely unclear. As the parents' desires are still important, he or she seeks to come to a "compromise among them, society's demands, and his own capabilities."[28] For an individual who falls under identity foreclosure, not experiencing a crisis and yet expressing a commitment are the identifying markers. Such an individual is becoming "what others have prepared or intended him to become"[29] and his or her beliefs closely follow those of the parents.

Propelled by Erikson's recognition and expansion of the psychosocial dimensions in identity formation and Marcia's identity status paradigm, subsequent research into the concept proliferated especially within the disciplines of sociology and psychology so much so that it underwent a process of diffusion and rapidly became a "cultural cliché and a technical term in [their] interpretive vocabularies . . . in the early 1980s."[30] For sociology, identity theory became the focus of research arising from sociologists' interest in the social nature of the self as a result of the roles that individuals occupy and interactions with others. Within psychology, social identity theory or identity arising from individuals' membership in groups emerged due to the discipline's interest in what happens to individuals. Thus, social identity is dictated by how individuals and others are categorized as in-groups or out-groups.[31]

Later Development

Identity Theory

Among the five different theoretical traditions in sociology, i.e., processual and structural symbolic interactionism, sociology of knowledge, structural-functionalism, and critical theory, identity became most prominently associated with structural symbolic interactionism or SI. According to Gleason, this association arose primarily due to SI's interest in the ways

---

28. Ibid., 552.
29. Ibid., 552.
30. Weigert et al., *Society and Identity*, 1. See also Ysseldyk et al., "Religiosity as Identity," 62.
31. Chen, "An Alternate View of Identity," 95–96.

"social interaction, mediated through shared symbolic systems, shaped the self-consciousness of the individual."[32]

While SI initially used self instead of identity due to the influences of George Herbert Mead and Charles Horton Cooley, identity took over as the stock term due to the important roles of Erving Goffman and Peter L. Berger in popularizing it through their works, which appealed to a wider audience. By moving away from Erikson's psychosocial frame of reference and considerably modifying the concept for the purposes of sociological analysis and generating a sociological frame of reference,[33] this process contributed to the deconstruction and diffusion of identity—marked by uncertainty in its meaning and a shift from what Erikson originally had in mind.

Viewing identity solely as an artifact of the interaction between the individual and the society, it is "essentially a matter of being designated by a certain name, accepting that designation, internalizing the role requirements . . . and behaving according to the prescriptions."[34] With individuals embedded within various role designations in society, their identity necessarily becomes many because society assigns them the various identities. With this socialization of identity, individuals do not exist apart from society.

Building on the notion of multiple social identities is Sheldon Stryker, who labeled his approach as "identity theory."[35] Subsequently, this theory has evolved to become one of the two main perspectives within the current research on identity.[36] Stryker argues that identity formation is critically affected by "larger social structural phenomena (e.g., community organization, class structure), which are presumed to operate essentially through commitment."[37] Thus, each individual or self is a structure of identities and

---

32. Gleason, "Identifying Identity," 917. See also Blumer, *Symbolic Interactionism*, 2; Cote and Levine, *Identity Formation, Agency and Culture*, 33. Blumer asserts that SI rests on 3 premises—we act on things that have meaning for us, the meaning is derived from interaction with others, and meaning undergoes transformation based on interpretations as we interact with our surroundings.

33. See Berger and Luckmann, *Social Construction of Reality*; Berger, *Sacred Canopy*; Berger, "Modern Identity."

34. Gleason, "Identifying Identity," 918.

35. See Weigert et al., *Society and Identity*, 21.

36. Chen, "An Alternate View of Identity," 95. See also Hogg et al., "Tale of Two Theories," 265.

37. Stryker, "Identity Theory," 89.

these identities are defined as "internalized sets of role expectations, with the person having as many identities as roles played in distinct sets of social relationships."[38]

Each of these identities varies in importance or saliency according to the degree of commitment that a person has to that identity. Stryker defines commitment as

> ... the costs to the person in the form of relationships foregone were she/he no longer to have a given identity and play the role based on that identity in a social network.[39]

In turn, commitment is dependent on the structures of society or social organizational principles (e.g., ethnicity, age) that will either facilitate or impede the entry and exit of the person from social relationships. Given this definition, the person is committed to a role based on the extent and intensity of social relationships.

Since commitment is equated with costs incurred for playing or not playing out a certain role, Stryker goes on to note that two types of commitment exist. The first is interactional commitment—i.e., the extensiveness of relationships arising from having a particular identity. The second is affective commitment, or depth of ties to the others based on an identity and the resulting "emotional costs attached to departure from a given role."[40] When the two types reinforce each other, the joint impact on identity salience will be significant.

While Stryker focuses on the hierarchical arrangement of identities within social structures and the impact of individuals' commitment upon their identities and salience, Peter Burke views identities as "self-meanings and that self-meanings develop in the context of meanings of roles and counter roles."[41] For Burke, identity behavior is a function of the "relationship between perceived meanings of the self in a situation and identity-standard meanings."[42] In other words, each identity held by an individual is tied to perceptions or a set of meanings that he or she attributes to himself or herself when acting out or claiming the identity.

---

38. Ibid., 90.
39. Ibid., 90.
40. Ibid., 98.
41. Stryker and Burke, "The Past, Present, and Future," 287.
42. Burke and Stets, *Identity Theory*, 55. See also Stets and Burke, "Identity Theory and Social Identity Theory," 225.

The set of meanings behind each identity defines the character of the identity and is known as the "identity standard."[43] According to Peter Burke and Jan Stets, this set of meanings behind identity standard is formed by three mechanisms—social learning, direct socialization, and reflected appraisals. Social learning refers to our observations and modeling of the primary or general culture in which we grow up.[44] Direct socialization is the formal and informal instruction we receive on what is expected when we take on a new role or identity. Finally, reflected appraisals are how we think that others are defining us.

Using these standards, which are relatively stable, as points of reference, individuals evaluate or verify the inputs or sources of information for our identities—i.e., our perceptions of our environment or meanings that we derive in a situation. Once these inputs are received, they are compared with the "meanings of the identity standard."[45] Based on the differences between the input and the comparator, an error signal is produced. This signal will then guide the output or the behavior in a situation, with the purpose of altering the environment from what it was.

While the sociological approaches, specifically SI as discussed above, generally conceive identity as socially constructed and variable, psychological approaches tend to look for the "locus of identity within the individual—as part of the psyche or 'inner workings.'"[46] Thus, for many sociologists, society *steers* identity formation, whereas for psychologists, it is the individual actively negotiating "among competing categories and groups in order to achieve psychological satisfaction."[47]

Social Identity Theory

Psychological satisfaction, which includes positive social identity, is the primary motivation that drives the social comparison process and the search for positive in-group distinctiveness.[48] This motivation is explicated in Henri Tajfel's social identity theory (SIT). SIT's usefulness is in providing

43. Burke and Stets, *Identity Theory*, 63.
44. Ibid., 63.
45. Ibid., 66.
46. Cote and Levine, *Identity Formation, Agency and Culture*, 48. See also Ashmore and Jussim, "Introduction," 6.
47. Deaux and Burke, "Bridging Identities," 316.
48. Ibid., 317.

new lenses to understand the "unarguably social nature of individual processes and the societal roots of human behavior."[49]

According to Marilyn Brewer and Miles Hewstone, social identity has two categories. The first refers to the aspects of self-knowledge arising from membership in specific social groups. In other words, social identities are aspects of the self that have been strongly influenced by participating in specific social groups or categories and "shared socialization experiences."[50] The emphasis here is the content of identity, which is made up of acquired psychological traits, expectations, customs, beliefs, and ideologies.

Second, social identity can also be defined as "the perception of self as an integral or interchangeable part of a larger group or social unit."[51] This understanding of social identity is best represented by John Turner's self-categorization theory (SCT), which explains how people become a group. Thus social identity is a "collective self . . . it is not an 'I' as perceived by a group, but a 'we' who are the group and who define ourselves for ourselves."[52] With SCT, new insights emerge on group formation and cohesion, social cooperation, crowd behavior, and de-individuation.[53] Thus, SIT and SCT are essentially the "inverse of each other, reversing the nature of the part-whole relation."[54]

For Henri Tajfel, an "individual's self-definition in a social context can be restated in terms of the notion of social identity."[55] Tajfel understands social identity as

> . . . part of an individual's self-concept which derives from . . . knowledge of . . . membership of a social group (or groups) together with the value and emotional significance attached to that membership.[56]

Based on this definition, Tajfel highlights three indispensable elements within SIT and four characteristics regarding group memberships.

---

49. Operario and Fiske, "Integrating Social Identity and Social Cognition," 30. See Thoits and Virshup, "Me's and We's," 107.

50. Brewer and Hewstone, "Introduction to this Volume," xi.

51. Ibid., xi.

52. Turner and Reynolds, "The Social Identity Perspective," 261.

53. Ibid., 261. See also Terry et al., "Group Membership, Social Identity, and Attitudes," 284.

54. Brewer and Hewstone, "Introduction to this Volume," xi.

55. Tajfel, *Human Groups and Social Categories*, 254.

56. Ibid., 255.

The elements, which interact together, include the need for a positive social identity, specific inter-group status differences in society, and responses to challenges posed to social identities based on their different locations in the social structure. The four characteristics are: (a) individuals will tend to remain a member of a group and also seek to be members of new groups if these groups contribute positively to their social identities; (b) if a group does not meet this requirement, individuals will leave unless there are reasons that make leaving impossible or if leaving will give rise to conflicts with personal important values; (c) if leaving a group presents the difficulties discussed above, then individuals may either reinterpret the attributes of the group so that its unwelcome features (e.g., low status) are justified or made acceptable or accept the status quo and engage in social action to bring about desirable changes; and (d) no group is an island—i.e., all groups in society live among other groups.

Studies on Religious Identity and Religion's Impact on Identity

The concept of religious identity is increasingly becoming a prominent theme in social science studies.[57] Its increasing popularity and development has been largely attributed to social scientists being increasingly cognizant of the strategic place and positive contribution of religion within sociocultural and interpersonal contexts.

Many of these studies have drawn heavily upon and extended the theories discussed earlier in this chapter. Besides Marcia, Hans Mol also expanded the work of Erikson and argued that identity be understood in light of religious beliefs and practices. For him, individuals have always looked for integration and identity, where the latter is defined as a "stable niche in this whole complex of physiological, psychological, and sociological patterns of interaction."[58] This stability is undergirded by religion or religious practices through the giving of "particular conceptions of order within a culture, thus making the security of the individual less precarious."[59]

---

57. For example Balkin et al., "Religious Identity and Cultural Diversity"; Bell, "Religious Identity"; Brubaker and Cooper, "Beyond 'Identity'"; Greenfield and Marks, "Religious Social Identity"; Peek, "Becoming Muslim"; and Tsomo, "Creating Religious Identity."

58. Mol, *Identity and the Sacred*, 8.

59. Ibid., 9.

Review of Theories of Identity and Religious Identity

Religion is thereby defined by Mol as the "sacralization of identity"[60] or a safeguard of the demand for sameness and order in the midst of encountering insecurity through engaging in four ongoing processes—objectification, commitment, rituals, and myths. Objectification is defined as the summing up of "variegated elements of mundane existence in a transcendental point of reference where they can appear more orderly ... consistent ... and timeless."[61] Commitment is viewed as an emotional attachment or fixation to a specific focus of identity—either in the form of ideas, people, or groups that create a sense of belonging. Ritual is the "repetitive, emotion-evoking action";[62] and myths point to the symbolic accounts or interpretations of "primordial conflicts"[63] between individuals and groups.

Dashefsky's purpose to provide "alternative conceptualizations of what the meaning of religioethnic identity and identification is"[64] arose from the ambiguities over the understanding of identity and identification that emerged due to the rising interest to anchor one's identity upon one's religioethnic background in the United States in the 1970s. For Dashefsky, identity is to be viewed "first as a higher order concept ... the sector of personal system that maintains ... continuity through coherent organization of information about the individual."[65] The information is derived from two sources—how others define the individual and how the individual defines himself or herself.

Identification, on the other hand, is both an active process upon which identity is elaborated, and a product of social interaction. For the former, it occurs when an individual links himself or herself to others in an organizational sense, formally or symbolically, with a person, group, or an organization. For the latter, arising from the process of linking, the individual's behavior and attitudes are guided by the lasting influence of the person, group, or organization.

Benjamin Beit-Hallahmi attempts to arrive at a more precise understanding of religious identity or religion as identity by integrating Erikson and psychological and sociological theories on identity formation. He puts forth three levels of conceptualizing identity—collective identity, social

60. Ibid., 1.
61. Ibid., 11.
62. Ibid., 13.
63. Ibid., 13.
64. Dashefsky, "And the Search Goes On," 239.
65. Ibid., 240.

identity, and ego identity. He argues that religious identity, or religion as identity, operates on the second level. On this level, it is "expressed by the individual and experienced by him as a label."[66] Thus, religion is "most often learned and acquired within the family"[67] and that only a small number of adherents have a choice of religious identity through exploration. In fact, religious identity—defined as "a distinctive group affiliation and respective beliefs"[68]—is not a matter of real learning but one that is ascribed to because of social location.

Shraga Fisherman's investigation of identity formation among adolescents draws upon Beit-Hallahmi, Erikson, and Marcia. Similar to Erikson's observation that religious identity is a source of support for ego identity,[69] Fisherman's research finds a positive correlation between spiritual identity and ego identity. At the same time, his model of religious identity development, which is based on an expansion of Marcia's Ego Status Paradigm, consists of three different levels—healthy, unhealthy, and dangerous.[70] Healthy development will lead to a consolidated and positive spiritual identity. Unhealthy and dangerous religious developments lead to diffusion, moratorium, and negative behaviors such as drug use and delinquency.

In a further study on another group of religiously observant adolescents, Fisherman further explicates the concept of religious identity. He notes that religious identity is (a) formed consciously or unconsciously by religious communities, (b) a subidentity related to social roles, and (c) a "source of support and integration for different portions of ego identity."[71] Furthermore it is made up of five dimensions—(a) experiential, or religious feelings, (b) intellectual, or knowledge about the religion, (c) ideological, or the beliefs, (d) ritual, or religious behavior, and (e) outcome, or the religion's effects. As such, this identity consists of both outward religious behavior and inward "religious orientation."[72]

Lori Peek's exploration of why Islam became the "most salient source of personal and social identity"[73] among young Muslims in America also

---

66. Beit-Hallahmi, "Religion and Identity," 86.
67. Ibid., 87.
68. Ibid., 87.
69. Erikson, *Identity*, 83.
70. Fisherman, "Spiritual Identity," 63.
71. Fisherman, "Ego Identity and Spiritual Identity," 373.
72. Ibid., 377.
73. Peek, "Becoming Muslim," 215.

points to a number of the above characteristics. In her analysis, the religious identity or religion as a social identity develops over three sequential stages—ascribed, chosen, and declared. It is acquired through social and developmental process. Thus, while the first stage is "taken for granted as an aspect of their individual and social selves,"[74] the other the stages were formed through the support of peers, self-reflection, or crisis events (e.g. September 11, 2001).

For Pamela King, religion is an important source for adolescents as they explore and form their identity. According to her, religion encompasses three contexts: 1) ideological (such as moral codes and values); 2) social (i.e., a faith community that offers spiritual modeling); and 3) spiritual (i.e. connectedness with divine or human). When the identity formation process is anchored upon these contexts, the resulting identity will be one "that transcends the self and can promote a sense of commitment that not only fosters individual well-being but promotes the good of society as well."[75]

In an attempt to understand if religious identity is shaped internally or externally among students at Carnegie Mellon University (CMU), Matthew Browne et al. found that "no identity-making process can be solely internal."[76] Defining religious identity as "people's ways of relating to a religion"[77]—which entails both the sacred or divine and the sociocultural community associated with the divine—they note that all the choices people make in choosing to be or not to be part of a religion or demonstrating their beliefs and how strongly they feel about their beliefs make statements about who they view themselves to be. At the same time, external pressures, such as those exerted by peers and hometown environment, influence these choices.

Another recent study specifically focused on religious identity is by David Bell. He adopted and extended Erikson and Marcia's psychosocial approaches by investigating how religious identity, as an "empirically unique, potentially separable component of identity (qualitatively different per identity statutes/stages," should be included as an "important measure when investigating degrees of religiosity (quantitatively different in salience to an individual)."[78] Bell sought to clarify the psychosocial functioning of

74. Ibid., 236.
75. King, "Religion and Identity," 197.
76. Browne et al., "Intercultural Inquiry of Religion," 1.
77. Ibid., 2.
78. Bell, *Religious Identity*, 7.

religious identity and construct a scale to measure religious identity and salience. For Bell, religious identity is simply "the way a person relates to a transcendent being or force and/or to a sociocultural group predominantly characterized by a transcendent object."[79]

According to Emily Greenfield and Nadine Marks, and Renate Ysseldyk et al.,[80] SIT serves as an invaluable framework to understand the relationships between individuals' membership or participation in social groups and their psychological well-being and responses to various circumstances. Categorizing religious identification or identity as religious social identity or a social identity anchored in a system of guiding religious beliefs that is seen as sacred, eternal, and unchanging, they argue that religious adherents hold to these beliefs tenaciously or participate actively in the associated religious practices. Thus, these acts become a powerful tool in shaping the psychosocial functioning of individuals, either for good (such as promoting emotional and physical well-being), or for evil (as in creating religious extremism and intergroup conflicts).

For Hopkins, the SCT provides an attractive model to overcome the inherent bias against minority faith identifications or identities (i.e., Muslim identity in Britain). SCT, which argues that social categories are as important in self-definition, can be used to analyze Muslims' participation in an ongoing process of renegotiating their religious identity in light of their social, political, and economic contexts.[81] Such an approach helps to guard against negative perceptions toward Muslim identity as invariant, thus enabling the possibilities of drawing upon religious identity as a resource to build social capital such as cohesion and trust.

In Tsomo's analysis, religious identity or identification informs the ways an individual perceives reality, and there are multiple sources that establish and maintain it. These sources include individuals assuming a religious identity according to the family's religious affinities, cultural reinforcement, social expectations, and a preference for social uniformity. Thus, shifts in religious identity or conversion will "inevitably involve shifts in one's identity as a whole"[82] through influencing how one is viewed by

---

79. Ibid., 11.

80. Greenfield and Marks, "Religious Social Identity," 246; Ysseldyk et al., "Religiosity as Identity," 60.

81. Hopkins, "Religion and Social Capital," 531.

82. Tsomo, "Creating Religious Identity," 81.

others and setting off changes in one's surroundings (e.g., relationships with family or friends).

Tsomo's research also provides insights into two facets of Buddhist identity. The first is the criteria for a Buddhist identity, which she states is to take refuge in the Buddha, the Dharma, and the Sangha. The second is her delineation of Buddhist theory of identity as comprised of the five aggregates of form, feeling, discrimination, karmic formations, and consciousness, and that the notion of identity "can be useful . . . in developing . . . a healthy and balanced sense of oneself in the world."[83]

Taoist identity receives an in-depth treatment in *Daoist Identity: History, Lineage, and Ritual*, which came about as a result of a three-day conference in New York to "discuss the difficult and . . . unexplored question of Daoist identity."[84] Acknowledging the plurality of identity in Taoism, the scholars did away with any "futile endeavor to find permanence and solidity in the tradition and begin by looking at identity as a process."[85] Instead they focused on the formation of identity within various areas of sacralization and specific situations—historical periods, schools, and local communities. Surprisingly, while they emphasized the plurality of Taoist identity, they summarized that Taoist identity is formed through certain general or typical patterns. The three major patterns include Taoist texts or scriptures, lineages affiliated with local and popular ideas and practices, and ritual practices. According to Kohn and Roth, these patterns match Mol's sacralization patterns of objectivation, commitment, and ritual.[86]

Discussion

The complexities of identity and the various facets associated with it have generated a plethora of literature that postulates divergent theories and approaches. However this review neither seeks to address all of them comprehensively nor resolves the existing chasms (e.g., synthesizing identity theory and social identity theory, problematizing identities). In line with the research topic at hand, this review is insightful in the following ways.

First, all the literature points to an individual's identity not being essentialist, or a given. Erikson and subsequent theorists advance the notion

83. Ibid., 78, 84.
84. Kohn and Roth, "Introduction," ix.
85. Ibid., 8.
86. Ibid., 7.

that individuals actively participate in constructing who they are in relation to others, society, and the world through social interactions. Regardless of whether individuals are seeking a positive social identity vis-à-vis the groups with which they interact, responding to peer pressure, or fulfilling the assigned social roles, these processes reflect active human participation in the process of establishing and maintaining identity.

Second, the literature highlights the significant role of external factors, such as sociocultural forces and interpersonal contexts of an individual (e.g., ethnic affinities, family-social relationships, religious communities or organizations) in establishing and sustaining identity. For example, Erikson points to an individual's communal culture as an anchor for identity while Marcia's statutes include assessment of parental influence and the impact of ideologies or beliefs. Both identity theory and social identity theory, and subsequent scholarship that utilize these theories, also highlight the critical contributions of groups or other cultures toward role identity or in-group identity.

Third, this review sheds insights into how religion can be a powerful tool in the identity-formation process of an individual. Metaphysical constituents of religions, such as rituals and beliefs/stories, serve to reinforce an individual's commitment to his or her religious identity such that the latter is not "easily dethroned and replaced."[87] Beyond these external forms, Fisherman's dimensions of experiential or religious feelings and King's spiritual context of religion (i.e., connectedness to the divine or sacred) highlight the potential and significant contribution of this inward religious orientation toward religious identity.

Finally, the surveyed literature provides an overview of the evolution in the understanding and definition of religious identity. While religious identity is currently subsumed as a part of social identity (e.g., Beit-Hallahmi; Greenfield and Marks; and Ysseldyk et al.) and thus "multiple, unstable, in flux . . . ,"[88] the above review has also called to attention the need to view religious identity as comprised of the overlapping but distinct entities of religion and identity. As such, the key characteristics associated with these entities, such as the element of stability, a sense of invigorating well-being that acts as a deep and abiding niche or identity standard for an individual over the course of his or her lifetime, and the impact of the divine or sacred toward establishing and maintaining the stability and rejuvenation,

---

87. Mol, *Identity and the Sacred*, 11. See also Kohn and Roth, "Introduction," 7.
88. Brubaker and Cooper, "Beyond 'Identity,'" 11.

must necessarily be integrated in order to sharpen our understanding of the notion.

While the above-discussed insights are useful, this review has also unveiled the following gaps within the current conceptualizations of religious identity. First, as noted in chapter 1, the current research into identity—religious or otherwise—has largely remained entrenched within the confines of Western scholarship and anchored upon an individualistic perception of identity. Thus, the establishing and sustaining of identity is primarily autonomous and egocentric in purpose—in order to assert self-uniqueness and location within society. Outside of the West, there is a paucity of qualitative research that seeks to discover and explain the dimensions that establish and sustain the religious identity of religious adherents.

Second, the conjoining of religious identity with social identity has led to a dearth of information in terms of (a) the reciprocal interactions between the adherents and the mysterious powers or the spiritual realities inherent in every religion, and (b) how the outcomes of these interactions contribute to the establishing and sustaining of religious identity. From the review above, it is evident that research is reticent to engage these facets in favor of verifiable and natural causes. Beit-Hallahmi goes so far to assert that, "Religious identity and religious beliefs are products of social learning. The whole research literature on religion attests to that."[89]

Even when an approach to understand the impact of transcendence or spiritual realities upon identity development is suggested, it has to begin with "norming existing measures that measure transcendence, such as the Spiritual Transcendence Index."[90] Yet, if the vibrant engagement with practices and rituals reflect religious adherents' sensitivity to, and dependence upon, spiritual realities in their daily practices and living,[91] then the insights gleaned from Singaporeans who are Buddhists or Taoists will contribute toward expanding the current research and enriching the insights within the larger body of theories by highlighting the significance of spiritual realities in establishing and sustaining religious identity

---

89. Beit-Hallahmi, "Religion and Identity," 87. See also similar conclusion by Kohn and Roth, "Introduction," 7–8.

90. King, "Religion and Identity," 203.

91. See case study by Heinze, in "The Dynamics of Chinese Religion," and Lagerwey, *Taoist Ritual in Chinese Society*, 286–87.

The Dimensions That Establish And Sustain Religious Identity

Third, there is a need to scrutinize the current conflated use of religious identity with religious identification or religiosity.[92] Brought about by the commonly accepted but diffused definition and understanding of religious identity, Rogers Brubaker and Frederick Cooper have labeled this phenomenon as the emergence of the "weak understandings of 'identity.'"[93] They assert that the use of the term is meaningless if it ignores the "everyday sense of 'identity' [which] strongly suggests at least some self-sameness over time . . . something that remains identical, the same, while other things are changing."[94] While this study does not agree with their call to abandon the use of the term, it does want to adhere to Gleason's call for a more concise understanding of the concept.[95]

Drawing from this survey of the theoretical landscape, it is likely that the dimensions that establish and maintain the religious identity of Buddhists and Taoists will encompass the contributory roles of external factors—i.e., various societal structures and cultural forces (e.g., role as a son or daughter, ethnicity, family, friends, temples, associations, fellowships) in Singapore. While these contributions are important, this study is focused on how these dimensions actually establish and sustain religious identity, especially vis-à-vis the role of the spiritual realities as revealed by the narratives of the Chinese Singaporeans who are Buddhists and Taoists.

Furthermore, by moving this research outside of Western confines, the emerging insights contribute toward enriching the understanding, establishing, and sustaining of religious identity. For example, the religious identity of Buddhists and Taoists is sustained by their desire to see blessings bestowed by the divine upon others instead of themselves. Furthermore, it is also possible that religious identity is established and sustained by the active role of sacred powers instead of societal factors. Finally, arising from the adherents' interaction with the sacred or spiritual, their experiences may further reveal the characteristics of wholeness, stability, rejuvenation, and belonging.

---

92. See Dashefsky, "And the Search Goes On," 243; Hiroshi, "Documents Used in Rituals," 256; Hopkins, "Religion and Social Capital," 528; Peek, "Becoming Muslim," 219; and Tsomo, "Creating Religious Identity," 77.

93. Brubaker and Cooper, "Beyond 'Identity,'" 10.

94. Ibid., 11.

95. Gleason, "Identifying Identity," 931.

Summary of Review

The key studies examined in these two chapters have provided an overview of how religious identity is currently understood and the dimensions that establish and sustain it. At the same time, these chapters have also described the existing gaps and how this study is able to address these gaps. The next chapter will describe my rationale and choice of research methods. The goal of these methods is to enable Buddhists and Taoists to articulate the dimensions that form and sustain their religious identity.

Chapter 4

Research Methods and Procedures

This chapter explains the research methods and procedures employed to achieve the stated goal of this study. I chose the qualitative approach for a number of reasons. These reasons can be classified into two main categories, namely: (a) the nature and context of my research topic, and (b) my underlying philosophical assumptions.

Reasons for Qualitative Research

Nature and Context of Research Topic

Despite the vibrancy of Buddhism and Taoism among Chinese Singaporeans, as discussed in chapters 1 and 2, the religious identities of Buddhists and Taoists remain inadequately researched. The resultant lack of clarity and research can be attributed to: (a) the current and common diffused definition, understanding, and use of religious identity, (b) the emergence of the majority of current research on identity—religious or otherwise—from a Western context, and (c) the emphasis on sociological constructs or typologies to explain how religious identity is established and sustained in studies emerging both from within and outside Singapore. In Sharan Merriam's opinion, qualitative research needs to be undertaken "when there is a lack of theory or an existing theory fails to adequately explain a phenomenon."[1]

Second, the dimensions that establish and sustain religious identity are often diverse and complex in nature. They include the observable

---

1. Merriam, *Qualitative Research*, 15.

dimensions, such as an expression of filial piety, family ties, or influences from society and religious community; and also the less observable ones, such as encounters or experiences with the divine. In order to obtain an in-depth understanding of these dimensions, I needed to situate myself in the world of the participants to hear their individual narratives and voices. I agree with John Creswell that these details can only be obtained "by talking directly with people, going to their homes or places of work."[2]

Third, my data collection entailed observing Buddhists and Taoists in their natural settings (e.g., temples, Dharma class, meditation sessions, and engaging in key rituals). Besides the narratives, these observations provided images and perspectives that a quantitative approach (e.g., filling out questionnaires) cannot capture. These images and perspectives proved to be immensely helpful when I analyzed my data to interpret the meanings expressed to me by the participants during the face-to-face interviews. For example, having been able to observe two classes (one in English and the other in Mandarin), I gained a deeper understanding of why a number of the Buddhist participants highlighted the teachings of Buddha as meaningful for their daily living.

Finally, predefined questions, as found in quantitative studies, are insufficient to capture the richness embedded within the religious experiences of the adherents. At the same time, any attempt to quantify the presence and work of the transcendent through any measurable scales[3] is absurd in light of the very nature of the divine. Thus, it is necessary to provide opportunities for the Buddhists and Taoists to recount their concrete experiences within their religions, observe the practices in which they engage, and to mine these sources of data to shed light on the dimensions that undergird their religious identity.

Underlying Philosophical Assumptions

Having delineated the nature and context of my study as factors influencing my choice of qualitative research in the previous section, I find it critical[4]

---

2. Creswell, *Qualitative Inquiry and Research Design*, 40.

3. As suggested by King in "Religion and Identity," using the Spiritual Transcendence Index, 203.

4. See Creswell, *Research Design*, 5; Merriam, *Qualitative Research*, 15; and Corbin and Strauss, *Basics of Qualitative Research*, 80, for analysis of how researchers' assumptions impact research design.

at this juncture to provide my background, philosophical assumptions, personal role, and interpretive paradigms before moving on to discuss my procedures of research.

Personal Background

I am a Chinese Singaporean who has lived in Singapore since the age of ten. Prior to that, I lived in Kuala Lumpur, Malaysia. Both of my parents are Christians, although my father grew up in a household that practiced an amalgamated form of Taoism/folk religion before he became a Christian as a teenager. While I have occasionally witnessed the rituals that my grandparents observed during festive occasions (e.g., Chinese New Year) in Malaysia, my parents have always explained to me why we do not practice them as Christians. At the same time, I also have many friends who are Buddhists or Taoists. While they have explained to me why they practice Buddhist or Taoist rituals, these occasions have been infrequent and their explanations brief. Thus, while I am emic in terms of my ethnicity, I am etic to the practices and beliefs of Buddhism and Taoism in Singapore. My philosophical assumptions are largely influenced by the Christian faith as propounded by my parents, and the churches and Christian organizations in which I have participated.

Personal Philosophical Assumptions

Creswell argues that in qualitative research, researchers make certain assumptions regarding the nature of reality (ontology), how the researcher knows what he or she knows (epistemology), the role of values in research (axiology), the language of research (rhetoric), and the methods employed (methodology).[5]

Ontology

Ontologically, I subscribe to critical realism, which affirms that there are features of reality "independent of our beliefs, perceptions or alleged knowledge of such,"[6] and also a world that is interpreted in various ways

---

5. Creswell, *Qualitative Inquiry and Research Design*, 16.
6. Potter and Lopez, *After Postmodernism*, 12. See also Bhaskar, *From Science to*

according to the experiences of the participants. It builds on positivism and instrumentalism, and assumes that knowledge or "truth of things-in-themselves does not necessarily . . . lie upon the surface."[7] There are two reasons why I hold to this position.

I hold to this position as it strikes a balance or middle ground between the presence of objective truth and that this truth is accessed or apprehended by different people in a variety of ways.[8] In my attempt to discover the dimensions or underlying structures that establish and sustain the religious identity of Buddhists and Taoists, this middle ground is critical for two reasons. On the one hand, it allows me to affirm that there are certain ultimate and undeniable spiritual dimensions within the world of Buddhism and Taoism. For example, my participants highlighted facets such as the intervention of 缘分 *yuan fen,* or destiny, in their lives, physical protection offered by the deities, and the 感应 *gan ying,* or resonance-response, given by Buddha when petitions were made to him for help.

Second, I cannot ignore the fact that relative or subjective aspects (e.g., personal experiences and emotions, cultural background and location) are also essential to the process of knowing,[9] because these cannot be avoided or eliminated in view of the complexities of the human phenomena.[10] The subjective aspects were expressed through the different experiences each of the participants had with the dimensions noted above.

While I agree with Norman Denzin and Yvonna Lincoln's observation that "objective reality can never be captured,"[11] such a position does not mean that a Christian researcher should abandon striving to more fully understand "the reality of the physical environment, . . . of human nature and psychology, . . . or of divine revelation."[12] I believe that through the faculty of reasoning and analysis with which we are endowed, it is possible to produce richly descriptive accounts of the complexities behind how Buddhists and Taoists in Singapore negotiate their religious identity.

Emancipation, 209.

7. Bhaskar, *From Science to Emancipation,* 209.

8. Ibid., 3–4. Critical realism began as a critique of positivism and against the "seeming incapacity of philosophies of science to really say anything about the world."

9. Potter and Lopez, *After Postmodernism,* 9.

10. Starcher, "Qualitative Research in Missiological Studies," 57.

11. Denzin and Lincoln, *Strategies of Qualitative Inquiry,* 7.

12. Kraft, *Christianity in Culture,* 22.

Epistemology

As a qualitative researcher, how I know what I know is through reducing the distance between the participants and myself.[13] This was why I chose to collect my data in Singapore. During the period of data collection, I made visits to various Buddhist and Taoist temples or organizations to interview different groups of adherents. These adherents were both introduced to me by the Buddhist or Taoist temples or organizations, friends, and also those whom I met randomly during my visits. During these visits, I also observed them as they engaged in religious practices or rituals in order to obtain a variety of firsthand information. According to Juliet Corbin and Anselm Strauss, the key reason for obtaining information from the participants is "qualitative researchers take with great seriousness the words and actions of the people studied."[14] Any explanation of people's experiences and the meaning assigned to those experiences is "incomplete without . . . locating experience within the . . . context in which it is embedded."[15]

This methodology of knowing stands in contrast to quantitative research, where the researchers "abstract from this world and seldom study it directly"[16] because their purpose is to test and not discover variables. Therefore, in Kathy Charmaz's opinion, the quantitative researcher is a "passive observer who collected facts but did not participate in creating them."[17]

Axiology

According to Creswell, qualitative researchers "admit the value-laden nature of the study and actively report their values and their biases."[18] As pointed out previously, my upbringing in a Christian family and critical realism influence my worldview.

---

13. Creswell, *Qualitative Inquiry and Research Design*, 247.
14. Corbin and Strauss, *Basics of Qualitative Research*, 14.
15. Ibid., 17.
16. Denzin and Lincoln, *Strategies of Qualitative Inquiry*, 16.
17. Charmaz, *Constructing Grounded Theory*, 5.
18. Creswell, *Qualitative Inquiry and Research Design*, 18.

Research Methods and Procedures

Rhetoric

Since I was the primary instrument for collecting data and analysis and my research involved entering the personal world of the participants, my writing style will be personal and narrative in order to better reflect what the participants revealed during the interviews. At the same time, the participants' voices will be prominent as they elucidate their personal interactions with the dimensions that establish and sustain their religious identity. Where there are terms that require additional definitions, I will draw primarily from what are provided by the participants with further insights elicited from scholarly research.

Method

According to Creswell, "the procedures of qualitative research, or its methodology, are characterized as inductive, emerging, and shaped by the researcher's experience in collecting and analyzing data."[19] Instead of using tightly prefigured categories (e.g., hypothesis, test instruments), qualitative researchers employ multiple interactive, emerging, and interpretive methods, and enjoy the "serendipity and discovery . . . making order out of seeming disorder"[20] as the research progresses.

Having designed an interview guide that consisted of open-ended questions (see Appendix A), I utilized it to frame my initial interviews. Drawing from the responses provided by the participants, I made edits to the interview guide (e.g., to include the use of religious terms regularly employed by Buddhists or Taoists) so that the questions became sharper in focus and subsequent participants understood them more clearly. As a result, I was able to fill out the gaps in my data during subsequent interviews—such as requesting the participants to provide an explanation for a phenomenon or a term. After each interview, I also listened to the recording a second time and reviewed the interview notes, with additional comments, missing information, or appropriate terms inserted into the latter.

---

19. Ibid., 19.
20. Corbin and Strauss, *Basics of Qualitative Research*, 13.

Role of Researcher

As the researcher is the primary instrument for data collection and analysis in the qualitative approach, Uwe Flick points out that a key aspect within the process is the subjectivities of the researcher (e.g., personal reflections, impressions, feelings and values).[21] What are the characteristics that helped me in my role as a qualitative researcher? I found Corbin and Strauss's suggestions[22] below helpful:

1. Curiosity
2. Creativity and imagination
3. The ability to recognize diversity as well as regularity
4. Willingness to take risks
5. Ability to live with ambiguity
6. Ability to work through problems in the field
7. Acceptance of the self as a research instrument
8. Trust in the self and the ability to see value in the work that is produced

As my research required me to work with various temples, associations, and participants whom I did not know previously (both introduced to me by temples, associations, or friends, and those whom I met randomly at the temples or associations), I would add that humility and cordiality are also critical. Thus, my research required me to bring my "whole self into the process."[23]

Since my research aim is hypothesis-generating, i.e., to discover and explain the dimensions that establish and sustain religious identity instead of hypothesis-testing, the questions I designed allowed those who participated in my research to share their stories, experiences, views, and knowledge. My interview sessions began with open-ended questions (e.g. "Why did you choose Buddhism or Taoism?") that helped the participants ease into the interview process. Subsequently, the continued usage of open-ended questions was critical to engage the participants and enabled me to gather the emic or insider perspectives.

---

21. Flick, *Introduction to Qualitative Research*.
22. Corbin and Strauss, *Basics of Qualitative Research*, 13.
23. Ibid., 13.

Research Methods and Procedures

Interpretive Paradigms

In bringing together my premises about ontology, epistemology, and methodology, I have created a paradigm or interpretive framework that guides my research. Creswell prefers to call it worldview, which he defines as "a general orientation about the world and the nature of research that a researcher holds."[24]

At the most general level, four major interpretive paradigms or worldviews structure qualitative research. Only the two that are related to this study will be described:

1. Social Constructivism: This position assumes each individual develops subjective and varied meanings of his or her experiences. The approach taken is inductive, generating a theory or pattern of meaning amongst the complexity of views presented by the participants.

2. Pragmatism: The focus of this position is on the outcomes or applications (i.e., actions, *what works,* solutions) of the research. The approach taken is to focus on the research problem and employ multiple strategies of data collection in order to derive implications that best address the problem.

In view of my research topic, I saw myself embracing the above paradigms. For social constructivism, a deeper understanding of the dimensions that establish and sustain the religious identities of my participants was heavily dependent on their perspectives. In terms of pragmatism, I concur with Corbin and Strauss's observation that an individual's choice to engage in research is to make a difference through the insights and understandings gleaned from the process.[25] For this research, the discovery and explanation of the dimensions will contribute toward (a) sustaining the peaceful religious climate in Singapore by providing other religious communities with insights into what establishes and sustains the religious identity of Buddhists and Taoists, (b) providing a more nuanced understanding of why Buddhists and Taoists continue to adhere to these religions, and (c) strengthening the current understanding of religious identity, as well as broadening the dimensions that establish and sustain it.

---

24. Creswell, *Research Design*, 6.
25. Corbin and Strauss, *Basics of Qualitative Research*, 11.

Reasons for Grounded Theory

As my purpose is to generate a theory that succinctly articulates and explains the dimensions that establish and sustain the religious identity of Buddhists and Taoists drawn from the diverse insights and experiences provided by the participants, the grounded theory approach[26] was most appropriate. At the same time, I also employed the systematic instead of the constructivist approach. The reason is, while I recognize that the data emerging from my participants reflected multiple realities, I do not agree with Charmaz that my findings remain inconclusive.

Through simultaneously using existing literature, drawing rich insights from participants that will best form my theory (i.e., theoretical sampling), and saturating the categories (i.e., data grouped together on similarities and tentatively given a label or name) that emerge, I can arrive at what Hiebert coins as approximate knowledge. Approximate knowledge "refers to knowledge related in one way or another to some reality or absolute."[27] While it may not be complete or exact, it does not render it relative or arbitrary.

Sampling Procedure in Grounded Theory

The sampling procedure in my grounded theory research is known as theoretical or purposeful sampling. During the time spent in Singapore, I reviewed each interview upon its completion—both by listening to the entire interview again and cross-referencing what I heard with the field notes that I took during the interview. I also did an initial coding of the data and created memos so that I was constantly aware of the aspects of the data that were being saturated and those from which I needed more information. Based on the evolving information derived this process, I then proceeded to either modify the interview guide or focus on a particular variance in terms of my sample (e.g., gender or years of practice) so that I was able to clarify the emerging categories and fill out the gaps.

---

26. See Charmaz, *Constructing Grounded Theory*; Glaser and Strauss, *Discovery of Grounded Theory*; Merriam, *Qualitative Research*; and Creswell, *Qualitative Inquiry and Research Design* for comprehensive description of grounded theory.

27. Hiebert, *Missiological Implications of Epistemological Shifts*, 92.

Research Methods and Procedures

Sampling Criteria and Participants in Grounded Theory

Creswell lists sixteen possible sampling strategies that qualitative researchers can employ. These include maximum variation, homogeneous, random purposeful, and convenience, among others.[28] For my research topic, I chose the maximum variation approach and was able to engage different participants (e.g., males and females, students, working adults, retirees) with different education levels (e.g., graduates, nongraduates, undergraduates) and in different sites (temples and Buddhist or Taoist organizations or associations such as a Buddhist Fellowship, Buddhist Library, or Awareness Place—a Buddhist bookstore located in a mall or Taoist Youth) to better capture a variety of perspectives. They include those who are long-time or recent adherents of the religions, from different educational backgrounds, engaged in different careers (e.g. homemakers, tertiary students, retirees, executives), males and females, and Mandarin and English-speaking Chinese Singaporeans.

In light of Buddhism and Taoism being the dominant religions among Chinese Singaporeans as pointed out in chapter 1, the criteria for my participants were that they be (a) Chinese Singaporeans who are Mandarin-speakers, English-speakers, or both; (b) adherents of Buddhism and Taoism who have been practicing the religions either for a long time (five years or more) or recently (five years or less); (c) from different educational backgrounds, i.e., current students, graduates, and non-graduates of institutions of higher education; (d) female and male adherents; and (e) in different occupations, such as tertiary students, bookshop employees, executives, retirees, and homemakers.

In terms of the number, it depended on the point of theoretical saturation, where no new information adds to my understanding of the existing categories. For this study, the sample size was thirty-two. It must be noted that the emphasis is not on the size of the sample but on how the sample can sufficiently help me to develop and explain my theory.

---

28. Creswell, *Qualitative Inquiry and Research Design*, 127.

Data Collection

Data Collection: Interviews

For this research, with permission granted by the temples, organizations, and the participants, face-to-face interview sessions were recorded on digital voice recorders and accompanied by interview notes. While an interview guide was employed to remind myself the areas that need to be covered in the interview, I had to remind myself that I should not become over-reliant on the guide—completing the questionnaires so much so that the interviews "shift from qualitative . . . to survey-style interviewing."[29] Instead, my focus was on their narratives and so I invited them to explain portions of the narratives that I did not understand (e.g., the process of transference of merits or the understanding of destiny).

Data Collection: Observations

Another data collection strategy that I used was observation. Corbin and Strauss point out, "The reason why observation is so important is that it is not unusual for persons to say they are doing one thing but in reality they are doing something else."[30] Furthermore, there may be participants who are unaware or unable to articulate the nuances in the teachings and practices of Buddhism and Taoism. Through observations and the notes taken, these gaps are bridged because I was able to use my observations to interpret the unclear aspects of the interviews.

However, as I am etic in terms of Buddhism and Taoism, I needed to check my interpretations of what I saw with the participants. Used together with interviews, observations would add rich dimensions toward my understanding of the factors that shaped the religious identities of my participants. During the period of data collection, I was able to observe: (a) an evening Mandarin *sutta* class conducted by a nun in one of the largest Buddhist temples in Singapore—the 光明山普觉禅寺, or Kong Meng San Phor Kark See Monastery; (b) a Mandarin *sutta* chanting session at 龙华禅寺, or Leong Hwa Chan Si Temple; (c) a meditation session for youths and Sunday service at Buddhist Fellowship (the Sunday service included the exposition of a *sutta*); and (d) offerings made to deceased ancestors by

---

29. Weiss, *Learning from Strangers*, 48.
30. Corbin and Strauss, *Basics of Qualitative Research*, 29.

various visitors during the Moon Cake Festival at a Taoist temple—三清宮, or San Qing Temple.

Literature Review and Use of Literature

Corbin and Strauss point out researchers "bring to the inquiry a considerable background in professional and disciplinary literature."[31] While there is no need to exhaustively review all literature in my field of research in view of the emergent nature of a grounded theory study (i.e., unexpected problems or concepts emerging from the data), familiarity with the literature has several advantages.

First, the concepts derived from the literature have been useful in helping me design my research questions and the interview guide so that I could use terms or concepts that the participants understood. For example, in my literature review, I found that societal structures—e.g., familial relationships, ethnicity, and temples—do impact the Buddhists and Taoists in Singapore. Thus, during the interviews, I explicitly asked the participants to explain how these have been helpful or not helpful in their continued practice of Buddhism or Taoism.

Second, a review of the literature has also been helpful in that I became familiar with the terms that they used during the interviews, albeit in English. While this approach worked for the common terms in English (e.g., Eight-fold Path, Triple Refuge, names of Taoist deities), it also proved to be a hindrance when the participants used the Mandarin equivalent. Thus, I had to ask for further explanation during the interview. At the same time, being etic also meant that such a review could not fully inform me of the varied subtleties existing in the religions as well as the range of the adherents' experiences with the metaphysical constituents. My lack of insider information meant that there was much to learn from the participants, which contributed to interview sessions that were enriching and meaningful.

However, Corbin and Strauss also warn the qualitative researcher against being "so steeped in the literature that he or she is constrained and even stifled by it . . . becom[ing] literally paralyzed."[32] While existing literature helped my research to maintain validity, I was mindful of using it as a guide instead of being controlled by it.

---

31. Ibid., 35.
32. Ibid., 36.

Time Frame, Length and Number of Interviews, Locations and Protocol

Data was collected in Singapore between September 4 and October 4, 2012. The length of each interview was approximately one hour. The number of interviews came to thirty-two. Theoretical saturation was reached at this point. The locations of the interviews were in places convenient for the participants (e.g., Buddhist Library, coffee shops, temple grounds, buildings where organizations are located). The observations were carried out in temples or buildings that the organizations rented for administrative purposes, worship sessions, and religious classes. Permission was sought from the temples and associations to gain access to these sites and from individuals to interview them and record the interviews.

Ethical Considerations

The participants were protected through three key measures. First, permission was sought from the Protection of Human Rights in Research Committee (PHRRC) through Biola University prior to the commencement of the interviews. Second, participants were given a consent form that informed them of the topic of my research—i.e., "the dimensions that shape the religious identity of Chinese Singaporeans as Buddhists or Taoists" and the interview process. For the participants who were not completely fluent in English, I provided a verbal translation of the entire form. Finally, I assured the participants that their views and identities would be completely confidential and would neither be revealed nor used in any manner to disparage any of the religions and violate any of the legal framework established by the Singapore government to ensure religious harmony.

Data Validation and Verification

Having collected and analyzed the data, how can I know if my account is valid and reliable? How do I verify my data? What and whose standards do I use? These are major concerns that must be addressed in my research.

Triangulation

According to Merriam, triangulation is "probably the most well known strategy to shore up the internal validity of the study."[33] The process involves "corroborating evidence from different sources to shed light on a theme or perspective."[34] Three common types of triangulation forms are regularly employed in qualitative research—use of multiple methods, multiple sources of data, and multiple investigators.

As I am not able to engage the use of other investigators in my study, I used multiple methods of data collection and multiple sources of data. The former includes interviews and observations while the latter includes data collected from different sites (e.g., temples, associations, public places) as well as other studies on Buddhism and Taoism in Singapore.

Member Checks

This is another common strategy to ensure internal validity or credibility. The key idea here is to "solicit feedback on [my] emerging findings from some of the people that [I] interviewed."[35] As the participants are emic in my research, I sent my first draft to them via email on October 13, 2013 to request their feedback by November 10, 2013. I also noted in my mail that if they did not provide any feedback by November 10, I would assume that what I wrote was unbiased and did not misrepresent what they told me during the interviews. A reminder email was subsequently sent out on October 28, 2013, which also extended the dateline to November 17, 2013.

Having not received any feedback after November 17, I sent out another email on December 4, 2013 to thank them for their help during the interviews and also to inform them that any further responses or feedback would no longer be incorporated into this research. Thus, I have taken the necessary steps to enhance the credibility of my research by providing opportunities for the participants to respond to my draft.

---

33. Merriam, *Qualitative Research*, 215.
34. Creswell, *Qualitative Inquiry and Research Design*, 208.
35. Merriam, *Qualitative Research*, 217.

Peer Review

According to Creswell, peer review or debriefing "provides an external check of the research process."[36] Here, I solicited the help of my peers from both the Cook School of Intercultural Studies and Rosemead School of Psychology to be the devil's advocates, asking "hard questions about methods, meanings, and interpretations."[37]

Reflexivity

Being reflexive in my research means reflecting critically on myself, clarifying my biases, philosophical assumptions, and past experiences at the beginning. These issues have been addressed in previous sections and help the readers understand how my values have impacted my approach to, and the conclusions of, my study.

Rich and Thick Description

Rich and thick descriptions involve providing detailed descriptions about the participants, settings, and findings in the form of "quotes from participant interviews, field notes and documents"[38] so that readers may be able to decide if the findings of my research are transferable. These aspects are demonstrated in chapter 5.

Audit Trail

An audit trail involves providing details of the "methods, procedures, and decision points in carrying out the study."[39] According to Corbin and Strauss, the provision of these details will convey the strengths and limitations of the study to the readers so they can assess "the analytic logic and overall adequacy or credibility of the research process."[40] The details are presented at various points throughout this study.

---

36. Creswell, *Qualitative Inquiry and Research Design*, 208.
37. Ibid., 208.
38. Merriam, *Qualitative Research*, 227.
39. Ibid., 229.
40. Corbin and Strauss, *Basics of Qualitative Research*, 309.

Adequate Engagement in Data Collection/Saturation

According to Merriam, adequate engagement with the participants and observations in the field are necessary in order to get as close as possible to their perceptions of the issue I am trying to examine. While it is difficult to predetermine the length of time or the number of participants, Merriam recommends that the researcher's data and findings must feel saturated—i.e., seeing or hearing the same things repeatedly and finding "no new information surfaces as you collect the data."[41] Even though the data collection and engagement with the adherents lasted only a month in Singapore, being an emic to the Chinese culture in Singapore having lived in the country for more than thirty years and spending the majority of my time during my field research by interviewing the adherents and visiting the temples or associations lessened the possibilities of miscommunication in terms of language and culture, and enabled me to understand the perspectives and stories of the participants.

Discussion

Qualitative research, in particular grounded theory, provided unique insights into the dimensions that establish and sustain the religious identity of Chinese Singaporeans as Buddhists or Taoists. At the same time, this approach has generated an overarching theory that succinctly summarizes and encompasses the dimensions as described by the participants. Furthermore, the methods and procedures adopted provided opportunities for the adherents to contribute their insights toward the research into religious identity, both in and outside of Singapore. The next three chapters will examine the theory and the accompanying major themes that emerged from the data analysis, with each major theme examined in a separate chapter.

---

41. Merriam, *Qualitative Research*, 219.

Chapter 5

Emerging Domain: Recognition

The purpose of this study is to discover and explain the dimensions that establish and sustain the religious identity of Chinese Singaporeans as Buddhists or Taoists. This chapter will present the theory, major themes, and findings that emerged from the analysis of the collected data. It will begin with a demographic sketch of the participants (see Table 1), before proceeding onto data analysis and the grounded theory generated from the analysis.

While the Buddhist participants included both long-time and recent adherents, none of the Taoist participants were recent adherents. Common answers given by the Taoists participants when I asked them "How long have you been in Taoism?" included "All my life since I was born into a Taoist family" or "Since young [i.e., as a child]."

Analysis of Data

Following my data collection, open coding produced seventy open nodes or categories that are related to this research. Subsequently, with axial and selective coding, six major themes emerged and these can be grouped into three dynamic domains—*Recognition*, *Appreciation*, and *Dedication* that undergird the proposed theory emerging from this study.

Emerging Domain: Recognition

Table 1—Demographic Data of Participants

Pseudonym	Gender	Education Level	Religion	Number of Years in Religion
PC	F	Graduate	Buddhism	5 or less
JK	F	Graduate	Buddhism	5 or more
AS	M	Non-graduate	Buddhism	5 or more
SL	F	Non-graduate	Buddhism	5 or more
JN	F	Graduate	Buddhism	5 or less
CK	F	Non-graduate	Buddhism	5 or more
CN	F	Non-graduate	Buddhism	5 or less
BD	M	Non-graduate	Buddhism	5 or more
MA	M	Graduate	Buddhism	5 or more
KSY	F	Undergraduate	Buddhism	5 or less
CW	M	Graduate	Buddhism	5 or less
YT	M	Graduate	Buddhism	5 or more
NY	M	Graduate	Buddhism	5 or more
JL	M	Graduate	Buddhism	5 or more
KS	M	Graduate	Buddhism	5 or more
BT	M	Non-graduate	Buddhism	5 or less
CT	F	Graduate	Taoism	5 or more
JH	M	Non-graduate	Taoism	5 or more
SY	M	Graduate	Taoism	5 or more
SYK	M	Non-graduate	Taoism	5 or more
KH	M	Non-graduate	Taoism	5 or more
YH	M	Graduate	Taoism	5 or more
LX	F	Non-graduate	Taoism	5 or more
KT	M	Graduate	Taoism	5 or more
KY	M	Graduate	Taoism	5 or more
MQ	M	Non-graduate	Taoism	5 or more
PH	M	Graduate	Taoism	5 or more
JE	F	Non-graduate	Taoism	5 or more
KL	F	Non-graduate	Taoism	5 or more
Group Interview of 3 (SW, KCL, YN)	F (All)	Non-graduate (All)	Taoism	5 or more
KC	F	Graduate	Taoism	5 or more

The central theory that emerged from the data and which best explains the dimensions that establish and sustain the religious identity of Chinese Singaporeans who are either Buddhists or Taoists is *The Enfolding*

Presence and Power of Spiritual Realities. This theory proposes that religious identity is established and sustained as the adherents come to experience the enfolding presence and power of these realities through immersing themselves in the dynamic domains of recognition, appreciation, and dedication (see Figure 1). Each of the domains is further undergirded by the subdomains respectively: (a) participation and revelation; (b) transformation, direction and protection; and (c) aspiration and obligation.

As the participants engaged in each of the domains, they sought to interact with the pervasive presence and power of spiritual realities, and very often, the reverse also happened (i.e., the spiritual realities interacted with the participants). Through these reciprocal encounters in these domains, the participants recognized and expressed their appreciation toward the well-being and help brought about by the presence and power of spiritual realities in their daily lives. Looking ahead to the future, they also expressed their lifelong dedication to these realities so that they are able to continuously experience a sense of well-being and also extend the benefits offered by these realities to those around them. The participants' sense of belonging and commitment to their religions are continuously reinforced through being immersed in these domains that sensitize them to the presence and power of spiritual realities.

Prior to a detailed explanation of the theory, it is helpful to elaborate on: (a) the enfolding presence and power of spiritual realities, (b) the dynamic domains of recognition, appreciation, and dedication, and (c) the subdomains associated with each domain. As pointed out in chapter 1, all religions attest to one or more of the following inherent metaphysical constituents—i.e., sacred beings or forces who are able to dispense spiritual health to humans and to whom humans can respond in a variety of ways,[1] as well as sacred texts and acts that cater to spiritual needs by providing insights to enable the transcendence of the biological selves, and unity and meaning to human existence.[2] Thus, for the adherents, these metaphysical constituents or realities surround them and continuously "fulfill [their] imagination and quest for an understanding of the unknown."[3] At the same time, the adherents seek to interact with these realities in their ongoing attempts to negotiate the tensions and anxieties associated with the present life and the life hereafter.

1. Tulasiewicz and To, "Religion and Society," 5.
2. Ibid., 5. See also Bidwell, "Practicing the Religious Self," 8.
3. Kuah-Pearce, *State, Society and Religious Engineering*, ix.

Emerging Domain: Recognition

Figure 1—A model of the enfolding presence and power of spiritual realities in establishing and sustaining the religious identity of Chinese Singaporeans who are Buddhists or Taoists (graphics by Melody Goh).

Both Buddhism and Taoism acknowledge the power and presence of these spiritual realities to benefit the living and the dead, and these realities exist in a continuum and communicate with the physical world.[4] Thus, in light of this acknowledgement, both religions encourage their adherents to aspire toward "moral and spiritual perfection, for authenticity, and for self-transcendence"[5] through a deeper understanding of the texts and engaging in a variety of acts—i.e., practices and rituals such as meditation, chanting, burning of offerings, and purification ceremonies.

For Buddhists, the affirmation of spiritual realities begins with the acknowledgement that Gautama Buddha attained spiritual awakening and has provided the Dharma and Sangha as guides for all Buddhists to realize this awakening. Thus, in taking the Triple Refuge, Buddhists demonstrate their confidence that "the Buddha, Dharma, and the Sangha . . . can help

---

4. Yu, "Merit Transfer and Life after Death," 43; Ching, *Chinese Religions*, 6. See also Hiebert's "Flaw of the Excluded Middle" for a Christian perspective.

5. Ching, *Chinese Religions*, 7.

... reach the truly satisfactory attainment of Nirvana."[6] Furthermore, Buddhists affirm that all of life's constituents, with the exception of *nibbana*, are marked by impermanence and dissatisfaction, or *dukkha*, as explained to him in the Four Noble Truths—which teaches that *dukkha* is the result of ignorance and craving. Thus, all Buddhists aspire toward *nirodha* ("cessation of creating suffering by refraining from doing things that make us suffer") and *nibbana* ("extinction of all notions . . . relative realities"),[7] thus obtaining release from the endless cycle of *dukkha*. In order to attain this spiritual goal, one needs to gain insights to lessen desires or cravings. These insights are gained through engaging the *suttas* and following of the Eightfold Path—i.e., to adopt right views, aspirations, speech, actions, livelihood, effort, mindfulness, and concentration.

Furthermore, the Buddhists also affirm the spiritual realities of *karma* and rebirth.[8] *Karma* is caused by the intentional actions of the body. With every action consisting of a cause and an effect, individuals engaging in good actions will bring about good *karma* while bad actions will bring about suffering. Thus, *karma* will determine if an individual will be reborn as a human or some other being. Buddhists strive to accumulate good *karma* through performing meritorious acts—such as observing the Five Precepts and doing good deeds—so that with each rebirth, they are able to move from the realms of desire and form toward the formless and a ceasing of desires in a future state of life.

While the Theravada school emphasizes individual efforts in attaining the spiritual goal through accumulated merits and correct understanding of reality, the Mahayana school points to availability of a *yana*, or vehicle, to aid individuals in the form of bodhisattvas, such as *Avalokitesvara* or *Guan yin*,[9] or *Maitreya*.[10] The bodhisattvas refer to those who have taken the vow to become a Perfect Buddha regardless of the number of rebirths for the benefit of all sentient beings. Despite experiencing enlightenment, bodhisattvas postpone their *nibbana* in order to help all sentient beings "in whatever ways may be of greatest benefit."[11] Endowed

---

6. Mitchell, *Buddhism*, 21.

7. Thich, *Heart of Buddha's Teaching*, 11, 137.

8. Mitchell, *Buddhism*, 9–10. This is the process of liberation. See also Gethin, *Foundations of Buddhism*, 216–17.

9. Tay, "Guanyin," 149.

10. Gethin, *Foundations of Buddhism*, 233.

11. Williams, *Mahayana Buddhism*, 58.

with such infinite compassion and wisdom, it is no wonder that they are the focus of meditation, reverence, and supplication on the part of adherents. In Chinese Buddhism, the two most popular bodhisattvas are *Guan yin pu sa* and *Amitabha*.[12]

As for the Taoists, they hold to the metaphysical nature of the *Dao*, or The Way, as "the primordial creative principle out of which the world came into being."[13] At the same time, it is also the anchor upon which *de*, or integrity, is founded upon through the former modeling 自然 *zi ran*, or "what is naturally so."[14] As a result, *Dao*, integrity, and nature become a "model for human behavior."[15]

Besides recognizing the importance of these facets, Taoism holds to a highly sophisticated pantheon of gods, goddesses, deities, and a complex system of ritual expressions. Both are viewed as important as the former is "perceived to be merciful and have a special regard for the people,"[16] and the latter is for "purification and renewal in the life-cycle and development of the human person"[17] so that adherents participating in them will be blessed with health, wealth, and longevity.[18]

Within the pantheon of gods, goddesses, and deities, a few are considered highly influential and thus popular among many Taoists. One of them is 妈祖 *Ma zu*, or Grand Old Mother. She is also officially known as 天后 *Tian hou*, or Empress of Heaven. The others include *Da bo gong* (particularly popular in Singapore), 关帝 *Guan di* (God of War), and *Guan yin*. Rituals, besides the regular 拜拜 *bai bai* (prayers or greetings offered to deities and/or departed ancestors) that adherents perform in their homes, are largely carried out by the 道士 *dao shi* (priests) or 乩童 *ji tong* (divining youth/shaman). The rituals are highly complex and all facets must be executed with proper formality. Thus, only the officiating priest or the shaman, who takes on the role of "an otherworldly bureaucrat,"[19] is able to procure the spiritual blessings for the community.

---

12. Lee, "Buddhism and Chinese Culture," 1.

13. Lee et al., *Taoism*, 91.

14. Ibid., 97. See also Khor and Chapman, *New Perspective on the Dao De Jing*, 15, 167.

15. Ching, *Chinese Religions*, 89.

16. Lee et al., *Taoism*, 118.

17. Ching, *Chinese Religions*, 115.

18. Lagerwey, *Taoist Ritual in Chinese Society*, 6.

19. Hiroshi, "Documents used in Rituals," 272.

The three domains of recognition, appreciation, and dedication are dynamic in nature due to the ongoing reciprocal interactions between spiritual realities and the participants within these domains—i.e., not only do the participants seek and interact with the spiritual realities, the latter also initiates interaction with the former. Furthermore, the dynamism is seen in how the domains impact one another. For example, recognition contributes toward appreciation, and appreciation has a role to play in dedication.

The recognition domain, which can be described as becoming aware or cognizant of the presence and power of spiritual realities, entails the subdomains of participation and revelation. Through participation (i.e., joining family members, friends, or 恩人 *en ren* (benefactors or, literally, persons of grace) in their regular observance of the practices or rituals in temples or their own homes), the adherents come to recognize and become aware of the prevalence and power of spiritual realities. As a result of this recognition and awareness, the participants pointed out that they knew which specific god or deity to turn to for different types of needs (e.g., *Guan yin* for sustenance during difficult times, or *Da bo gong* for ensuring things go smoothly at work or in business), and what to do during difficult times, such as *bai bai*, meditate, and read the *suttas*.

Revelation is distinguished by the participants' encounters with the intersection of *yuan fen*, or destiny, in their lives, manifestations (e.g., appearance of gods, goddesses, or deities in dreams), and miraculous acts. While the theme of participation reveals how the participants came to recognize the power and presence of spiritual realities by following family or friends to engage in the practices or rituals, the revelation theme demonstrates how the participants personally encountered the power and presence of the spiritual realities as these realities made their presence known in the daily experiences of the participants. The impact of these revelations is so significant that they became powerful motivating forces to sustain the commitment of the participants as either Buddhists or Taoists.

The second domain is appreciation, where the participants expressed their gratitude toward the presence and power of the spiritual realities because of the ways the spiritual realities helped the participants. Three subdomains emerged within this process—transformation, direction, and protection. Transformation points to the inward renewal brought about by the participants' realization of the existence of these realities. As a result of seeking the help of these realities during difficult times by engaging in practices and rituals such as meditation, chanting, listening to or reading the sacred texts, and petitioning to the Buddha or gods for help, they gained strength and sustenance that enabled them to overcome periods of crisis, such as depression and grief, and negative behaviors or attitudes (e.g., being ill-tempered, harboring hate).

At the same time, the participants also expressed their appreciation toward the teachings found in the Buddhist *suttas* or the *Dao de jing* that provided them with direction for life. Transmitted through classes regularly conducted at temples or associations and different forms of media easily accessed at these places (e.g., DVDs, CDs, free pamphlets or books), the teachings endow the participants with spiritual insights to understand the realities that exist beyond the physical world and the present life (e.g., impermanence of all things, workings of the universe, existence of other beings, levels of hell) and spiritual principles to live by in view of these realities. These serve to give direction to the participants (how to live during this life in preparation for the life to come).

Besides being appreciative of the transformation and direction that they received, the participants experienced the physical protection provided by the presence and power of the spiritual realities. From the interviews, I learned that the participants and their family members experienced physical well-being (e.g., recovery from physical ailments and being delivered from harassment by an evil spirit) through (a) engaging in practices such as *bai bai*—which encompasses the participants praying for safety and health on behalf of family members and themselves, and requesting the intervention of the gods to ensure a successful operation for a family member, or (b) inviting the 乩童 *ji tong*, or divining youth/shaman, to perform cleansing rituals.

Even as the participants expressed their appreciation of the transformation, direction, and protection brought about by the enfolding presence and power of these realities inherent in Buddhism and Taoism, more than half of them also highlighted their disagreement over how Christians in Singapore (a) responded to the physical representations of these highly regarded realities through their actions, and (b) presented their spiritual realities; for example, an overemphasis on forgiveness and that believing in Jesus Christ will result in salvation and rejecting him will bring about damnation. Thus, this subdomain is insightful in that it reveals how the participants' appreciation of the spiritual realities within Buddhism or Taoism is strengthened by their disagreement with the words and actions of Christians during proselytizing or preaching during Sunday services.

In the third and final domain of dedication, the participants expressed how the presence and power of spiritual realities serve to inspire them to remain as life-long adherents of Buddhism and Taoism. Although a number of the participants reiterated the subthemes associated with recognition (i.e., participation and revelation) and appreciation (i.e., transformation, direction, protection, and disagreement over actions and words of Christians), many of them also provided other reasons for their continued commitment to these religions in the days ahead. Two subdomains, which revolve around their ongoing attempts to strive toward higher spiritual goals of realizing the insights gleaned from the sacred texts into their lives, and to extend spiritual well-being to others (e.g., family, friends, and humanity) in the days ahead, undergird this domain. These subdomains are aspiration and obligation.

For many of the participants, aspiration is characterized by the commitment to strive toward continuous personal cultivation for inner wholeness, well-being, and benefiting others because of this cultivation. Other participants highlighted their aspiration as seeking to help others gain freedom from the cycles of births and rebirth, deepen their understanding of the Dharma, and resolve the daily issues and anxieties through dedicating themselves to become a bodhisattva, nun, or lifetime assistant to a divining youth.

Obligation points to the adherents' attempts to seek spiritual well-being bestowed by the power of spiritual realities for their family members out of filial piety. Obligation also serves as a means of alleviating the tensions and anxieties associated with what lies beyond death—e.g., endless rebirth cycles and hunger. Thus, the participants commit themselves to accumulating merits through various endeavors (e.g., copying *suttas* such as 普门品 *Pu men*, or Universal Gateway Chapter of the Lotus *sutta* associated with *Guan yin*, practice *metta*, or lovingkindness). These merits are both for themselves as well as to be 回向 *hui xiang*, or transferred to others (both living and deceased) for the attaining of enlightenment. Besides these merit-accumulating endeavors, others include regular offering of food and necessities (e.g., *jin zhi*, or notes to be used in the nether world, paper-made cellphones, shirts, etc.) to deceased ancestors during significant occasions (e.g., festivals and death anniversaries).

For the remainder of this chapter, I will examine in detail the recognition domain and the entailing subdomains.

Emerging Domain: Recognition

Recognition of the Enfolding Presence and Power of Spiritual Realities

This domain emerged from what the participants described as encountering and learning about the presence of spiritual realities enfolded within the symbolic forms and activities (e.g., chanting, meditation, offering of joss sticks) in Buddhism or Taoism, or in face-to-face meetings with these realities as the latter revealed themselves to the participants. As noted earlier, spiritual realities entail sacred beings, texts, and acts. The two subdomains that undergird this process are participation and revelation.

Participation

"Follow parents," "being around friends," and "born into a family" are key phrases that were repeated by many of the participants when they described their first realization of the spiritual realities embedded within Buddhism or Taoism. Being immersed in environments that consisted of family members or friends who either actively engaged in regular rituals in temples or in their own homes, many of the participants mentioned that they came in contact with Buddhism or Taoism as they participated in rituals or practice alongside family or friends.

Family

BD, who has been a Buddhist for over twenty years and took the Triple Refuge three years ago, described how he came into contact with various Chinese gods and deities as a result of being in an environment in which his parents and friends *bai bai* to the deities or gods:

> In the beginning, parents adhere to *bai bai*, so in this area . . . we naturally came into contact with . . . Buddhism. This is the first point. The second point is the friends around me are Taoists and there are also Buddhists. So naturally, I came into contact with Buddhism . . . this kind of faith. So it was from here that I started believing.

For SY and MQ, both Taoists for more than fifty years, they recalled with fond memories how their parents and fellow villagers brought them along to participate in the various rituals and festivities at the Taoist temples. Through this ongoing participation, seeking the help of or simply venerating the deities and gods through *bai bai*, became a lifelong practice:

SY ... from young, in the *kampong* [or village] district, it is like there were Taoist temples ... when there were Taoist temples, naturally we will participate in the activities there ... *bai* to the gods, burn joss sticks. We just followed these and continued on ....

MQ Can say it is family ... because on different festivals, we have to perform rituals. When my mother was still alive, we have to follow her to perform ... have to help, you have to follow her to do ... all these. So, we become used to it ... like for example, even after we got married, at home we still have to perform .... That is to say, on different festivities, have to *bai bai* or whatever ... say when do we have to *bai* ancestors ... so holding on ... holding on ... it became a few decades.

Through following their parents to visit the temples or assisting them in the preparation of the items needed for *bai bai*, the participants became aware of and recognized the pervading presence and power of spiritual realities such as Buddha, gods (e.g., *Guan yin, Da bo gong, Guan di*) whom they could turn to for specific needs, and key rituals and practices (e.g., *bai bai*, meditation, 念佛 *nian fo*, or chanting the name of Buddha) that needed to, or could be, carried out regularly.

Friends

Apart from being immersed in the familial environment, the participants also acknowledged the important role of friends or colleagues who are Buddhists or Taoists in pointing them to the religions or helping them to be better adherents. An interesting insight I gained from the Buddhist participants when they talked about these friends they got to know in classes or temples is the different terms used to describe these friends, such as *kalyana mitras* (spiritual friends), 佛友 *fo you* (friends in Buddha), and 恩人 *en ren* (benefactors).

For example, SL and JN recalled how friends played the role of benefactors and guided them to Buddhism. As for BD and BT, they highlighted the critical role of friends in Buddha who helped them to gain more insights into the teachings as well as encouraged them to persevere in Buddhism. KSY, who is currently pursuing her degree overseas, described how she missed the support of her *kalyana mitras* in Singapore. Without their support, she noted that her Dharma practice often was lacking while overseas.

At the same time, it is also important to note that the recognition of the presence of spiritual realities via the initial participation did not remain passive. Arising from the initial recognition, the participants went on to proactive participation whereby they sought to (a) find out more about Buddhism and Taoism, or (b) turn to the spiritual realities for help during difficult phases in their lives.

For a number of the Buddhists, they pointed out that their first contact with the enfolding spiritual realities within Buddhism through their parents was unhelpful in the sense that their parents are "joss stick Buddhists"—a phrase that they used to point to a nominal and ritualistic practice of Buddhism. Both MA and YT echoed these sentiments:

MA I see my parents ... they are just joss-stick Buddhists ... so I feel that with those real teachings of the Buddha ... so I feel that it will actually benefit them.... It will sort of actually make them maybe happier ... you know ... to understand what is the real teaching about....

YT Ya ... because most of the exposure to Buddhism, even when I was young, my parents were just nominal Buddhists, whereby they go to a temple to burn joss sticks and ... A lot of chanting, and even when you go to temple, you just pray and just walk away. So to me that is [Buddhism] ... Ok ... before I get to know more [about the teachings]... six years ago, right.

KS also expressed similar thoughts based on his past encounters with Buddhism:

> In Mandarin [i.e. amongst Mandarin-speaking Chinese Singaporeans] we say "Buddhism is only about performing Dharma or purification rituals. It only does these things." But I say this is wrong. Buddhism is not about doing these things. True Buddhism is not like that. But in Singapore, unfortunately, they all doing this kind of thing ... ya.

As a result, they stated that they were motivated to seek and return to a "more original form of Buddhism"—i.e., one that is closer to Theravada Buddhism and focuses on the "real teachings of Buddha" instead of the masters (e.g., as in Mahayana or Vajrayana or Tibetan Buddhism).

With the help of their friends, they came into contact with what they termed as a "more original form of Buddhism" and found the spiritual insights put forth by the teachings of Buddha to be extremely attractive and helpful. MA, YT, and CW shared their own journeys:

MA So basically I find that Buddhism is more . . . you know . . . logical . . . it makes sense and like things which is quite true . . . . Like I mean sufferings and impermanence and of course the way they view life and everything . . . so this is how I got attracted. So I think he [a friend] is the one to actually like lead me to the right . . . the so-called the more knowledgeable-based Buddhism that we are talking about . . . , rather than just going through those . . . you know . . . those rituals-sort of Buddhism . . . ya.

YT . . . if you look at the Buddha's teachings, a lot of the teachings are talking about happiness . . . in search of happiness and how to be happy . . . you see. So, by applying what he taught 2500 years ago, and those things that he taught is still very practical in our daily life. Talking about kindness, talking about letting go . . . talking about how . . . how the craving, you know, wanting things that causes a lot of suffering. So by being equanimous, by understanding the nature of life . . . that actually helps to be more calm and also be more understanding, right.

CW The true teaching of Buddha . . . it means that it is teaching me the way of life. How to handle daily issues, it is not just the mundane stuff but also the supra-mundane stuff [mundane points to the phenomena in the world, such as matter, consciousness, evil, virtue; and supra-mundane is that which transcends the world, e.g., nirvana, paths leading to nirvana]. Of course, to get onto that, I have to understand the mundane first.

Similarly for the Taoists, with the help of friends from Taoist Federation, a number of them also moved beyond their initial practices of Taoism as being confined to 神坛 *shen tan*, or altars built for gods, 庙宇 *miao yu*, or territorial temples,[20] the ritual of 跳童 *tiao tong*, or shamanic dances performed by divining youths, and the use of 咒 *zhou*, or mantra-like chants. Presently, they are learning more about the doctrinal underpinnings of Taoism as found in the *Dao de jing*. JH, a Taoist for about thirty years, described his own journey as:

---

20. Ichiko, "Manifestations of Luzu," 185.

Emerging Domain: Recognition

...before that, it is due to my parents *bai* the gods, we also follow and *bai* the gods. During our generation, it has always been like that. In 2007, I got to know Taoist Federation. Here, I...have learnt quite a lot of things—such as knowledge. Then...then I found out that "Eh...the original meaning of Taoism is like this." Before this, it was ....when I joined Taoism, it was at the other *shen tan* or *miao yu*. They have *ji tong*...in Hokkien they say *tiao dang* or *tiao tong*. Then it is like...I thought this is...that gods are like that. Eventually, when I came to Taoist Federation, I found out that actually these...are a form of folk religion. The original Taoism is...what is known as...started from the *Dao de jing* ...that is to say it is related to reading the books.

Similarly for YH, who recently decided to seek a more in-depth understanding of the *Dao de jing*, described his decision to join the Taoist Youth:

> I think...because I feel that in my *shen tan*, what I am learning there is insufficient...insufficient depth...I only learnt...what was on the surface...learnt to chant *zhou*, draw the charms ...but the true...deeper...going to a deeper level...so I feel that maybe I should join the Taoist Youth...I hope that from there, I can see what Taoism, inside it, what it is like. Is it only solely shaman's dancing in a trance, divining youths, drawing of charms, chant *zhou*? Or are there other aspects? I think it is not solely about shaman dancing in trance only. That is why I hope that by coming here, I can learn more.

Besides investigating more about their religions, the participants also acknowledged that by having been introduced to the presence and power of spiritual realities via participating in rituals or practices alongside family or friends, they knew instinctively to seek the help of these realities during times of crises in their lives. JL, YT, and KH recounted their experiences:

JL   It is just that...probably due to the upbringing as a...in a ...in a traditional Taoist/Buddhist family...it is natural to maybe seek solace in the religion that you are most familiar with...ya ...that's what I feel.

YT   ...Six, seven years back...I am undergoing some period of stress. To be precise...I think it is more like mid-life crisis...So there are a lot of suffering in my life. I mean there are a lot things going "Why am I here?"...there are questions you see. So...but way back twenty years ago, when I was in the university, there was some friends who passed me a book about Buddhism . . . talks about the teachings and all these things. So that suddenly came up in my mind . . . so I thought maybe there are some solutions or some answers. So that's where I start to seek the answer.

KH In what I experienced, something that happened recently, my father contracted colon cancer . . . last year, he contracted colon cancer. I don't expect much . . . I only asked the gods and deities . . . I hope that he will be healthy . . . to be able to pass through this stage . . . because from what the doctor said this is not a good . . . not a very ideal situation . . . the operation was also not going to be too ideal . . . chances of success is 50-50. Then what can we do? We pray to and ask the gods and deities . . . protect, that is to say, father be healthy and pass through this difficult stage.

Other forms of crises experienced by the participants or their loved ones, a few of which are more severe, included nightly disturbances by a malevolent spirit, the collapse of a business venture, depression and thoughts of suicide as an adult due to physical abuses suffered as a child, divorce arising from husband's infidelity, and sudden and unexpected deaths of a participant's older sister and father-in-law. In the midst of these situations, the participants expressed that knowing whom to turn to for help resulted in them finding the necessary answers or solutions.

AS's personal journey reveals how he turned to Buddhism in the midst of his depression because a friend introduced him to the Dharma:

I grew up in . . . an unhappy family. My parents were quarrelling constantly. Father would hit and scold us . . . hit and scold us . . .which is difficult to understand as he would hit and scold us without any reasons. Thus, I was emotionally scarred. Later on, when I was twenty-seven to twenty-nine years old, I felt I was abnormal . . . had depression. If I had continued on, no one was able to help me. There was only one road for me—to take my own life. Thus I saw the need for the faith from a religion to save me. Then I came into contact with Buddhism . . . there was a friend who once helped me. He once studied in a Buddhist school . . . he knows a bit of Dharma . . . teachings by Buddha. Then when I felt lost or depressed, he would tell me a little about Dharma. From there, I entered into a kindergarten [i.e., beginning] stage . . .

As for KSY, she recounted that her mother's personal walk as a Buddhist and past efforts to bring her to various Buddhist rituals while she was young left a deep impact on her in terms of recognizing the usefulness of Buddhist rituals and practices in coping with the stress of daily life:

> ... so for me, my mum was a Buddhist. So since young, I had ... I went for Buddhist rituals and whatnot. So that ... and I kind of see how Buddhism actually helps her a lot in life. My mum is generally quite a chill person and ... I think ... she could cope with lots of things in life. She does well and she can cope with all the stress and whatnot. I kinda admire for that ... and I honestly think that Buddhism helps her a lot with that ...

Recognizing the presence and power of sacred realities via participation (i.e., being introduced to and included in the practices and rituals undertaken by family members or friends) is an important experience that the participants underwent as part of their growing up in their social environments. This recognition can be viewed as the starting point in establishing their religious identity. At the same time, the recognition domain also served as the foundation for their lifelong commitment to their respective religions. It is also important to point out that although the recognition took place via the participants' respective social environments or structures, these environments served primarily as conduits for them to encounter and be sensitized to the presence and power of spiritual realities.

Subsequent to the initial recognition and encounters, the participants proactively sought to learn more about these realities embedded in the religions or the help of these realities during times of personal crises. The appreciation domain emerged as a result of participants experiencing and benefitting from the help afforded by the power of these realities (e.g., teachings, interventions by gods or deities). Prior to a more complete discussion of the appreciation domain, the remainder of this chapter will investigate the participants' recognition of the presence and power of the spiritual realities via revelation.

Revelation

The key characteristic of the revelation subdomain is spiritual realities taking a proactive role to make themselves known to the participants. The majority of the participants acknowledged that they encountered sacred beings or some form of divine force. Even though the participants acknowledged that these experiences were mysterious, they were neither shocked nor surprised by these revelations. For a few participants, they even described the experiences as 順 *shun*, or what is natural.

Destiny

For many of the participants, a key form of revelation that intersected with their lives is *yuan fen*, or destiny. Contrary to the Western perception of destiny as equivalent to fate, and thus possessing negative connotations—i.e., inability of someone to escape from it—the participants viewed destiny as a positive force that guides and takes care of them in this life. One of the ways that destiny carried out this role is guiding the participants to come into contact with Buddhism or Taoism in this life.

In the participants' perception, destiny is the result of the accumulation of good merits or *karma* over the course of individuals' past lives. Furthermore, destiny is also attributed to the practice of Buddhism in their previous lives. In their present lives, destiny naturally guided them toward Buddhism. Third, destiny can also arise as an individual keeps in step with or abides by life's spontaneous occurrences.[21]

Participants CN, BD, BT, YH, LX, and AS attributed destiny's active role in their present lives as a result of the accumulated merits from their past lives:

CN For one to be a Buddhist or to learn Buddhism . . . we need to accumulate merits for the past, previous life or a few lives before to have this destiny or primary or secondary causes to study or to get in touch with Buddhism. So I believe so that this destiny . . .

BD Well, we believe in our previous life, we were all Buddhists . . . we have been practicing. So somehow this understanding of Buddhism is deep inside us.

BT Why did I choose Buddhism . . . it is because . . . it is . . . sometimes when discussing about this . . . it is a form of destiny . . . like that. It is not because someone recommended it. It is . . . when your parents passed away . . . both of them passed away. Next to the housing estate where I live, actually there is a temple. This temple has actually been there for about 15 years . . . from the time we first moved to the housing estate until now. We do not intentionally visit a temple. Since . . . since the death of mother, then coincidentally I

21. Lee et al., *Taoism*, 98.

Emerging Domain: Recognition

walked into the temple . . . Yes . . . this is called destiny with Buddha . . . destiny with Buddha. Unless there is someone who invited you to go there, or your own friends bring you along, usually this type of opportunity and destiny is very rare . . .

YH   Something like that [destiny] . . . Because realistically-speaking, the birthday of the god in the temple matches with my birthday . . . as in Chinese calendar . . . the god is *Qi tian da sheng* [Great Sage, Equal of Heaven, Monkey God] . . .

LX   For me, I think that it is destiny that brought me into Taoism . . . or . . . brought me into this family and this religion. Because like without this destiny right, I won't get to know WY, my friend, and WY won't be . . . offer me a job. I used to work here. . . so he offered me a job here. Then without coming here to work, I won't be able to meet my fiancé . . .

AS   To put it briefly . . . it is also . . . maybe here I . . . during this time spent together with them, I think it is very natural. That is to say it is very smooth. The most important thing is to have this destiny. I think that they "Eh . . . it is not difficult to interact with them." Moreover the young people here very friendly. The way they think is very good . . . thus I am able to be accepted here for so many years . . . it is like this.

For YT, he pointed out that his inherent ability to understand Buddhism is due to his practice of Buddhism in his previous life:

> Well, we believe in our previous life, we were all Buddhists . . . we have been practicing [Buddhists]. So somehow this understanding of Buddhism is deep inside us. And when we heard something that is not quite in line with your . . . so called your consciousness, you don't seem to be able to gel in at all, you know . . . one of the monk did say that . . . a Western monk . . . he was telling us that he was born in a Catholic family as well. So when he was young . . . same thing . . . similar thing . . . when he go to church with his mother, doesn't seems to gel in at all. And then when he went to university, he did a study in Buddhism, and then it seems that "Eh . . . this one sounds right" . . . you know. So much so now he is a monk.

KC, a Taoist, along with a number of other participants also pointed out similar sentiments of the inability of the teachings of other religions to "gel in"—especially in understanding "the gospel sharing." They often used phrases like "doesn't go into me," "does not make sense," and "not logical."

Thus, for the participants, destiny has always looked out for their well-being by guiding them to encounter Buddhism or Taoism and enabling them to understand the teachings of these religions. For me, being etic to these two religions, I was surprised in terms of how attuned the participants are to destiny's active guidance and participation in their lives. Amidst the presence of societal influences, the participants were able to pinpoint the moments that destiny revealed itself.

This recognition led them to a lifelong commitment to these religions because they pointed out that since destiny blessed them by bringing them into contact with these religions, it is also important for them to continue to 随缘 *sui yuan*, or to be in step with, destiny for the rest of their lives. For BD, he noted:

> That [*sui yuan*] is a good phrase . . . it is a kind of destiny. . . Then I continued with this journey till now . . . I deeply believe that this road that I have walk is not wrong. So thus I will continue to walk in it.

Similarly for SYK and LX, their commitment to continue in Taoism is simply to continue to follow the path of destiny. SYK summed it up well by stating:

> But I will do until I can do no more because my physical health is a problem . . . I know myself. Thus, I will do until my last breath . . . do until I cannot move and then that is the end. Follow the path of destiny . . . I always say *sui yuan* [be in step with destiny] . . . really.

Manifestation

Besides destiny, another important form of revelation is the manifestation of the presence and power of spiritual realities. The manifestation described by the participants occurred in various ways—dreams, force, stimulus and response, and miraculous acts. For a number of the participants, these manifestations reaffirmed their destiny with the respective religion.

The Taoist participants were especially vivid in detailing the various gods, goddesses, and deities who appeared to them in their dreams. Below are various examples of who appeared in their dreams. For Participant JH, he described his encounter, which he also attributed to his destiny, with a popular but impulsive child-god in Taoism known as 哪吒, or Nezha:

> I dreamt about a god who we have in Taoism, known as 中坛元帅 *zhong tan yuan shuai* [Grand Marshal of the Middle Altar or Nezha] . . . it was very mysterious. In front of me . . . he went up . . . *zhong tan yuan shuai* . . . Nezha . . . 三太子 *san tai zi* [colloquially known as the Third Prince] . . . It was very mysterious . . . he . . . because last time we thought . . . the dressing of the gods. . . is it like this, like the 净身 *jing shen* [or pure body, a term Taoists use to refer to the statue of the deity] in the temple? It was really like what we *bai* in the temple . . . his dressing was exactly the same. So from then on, I believe in Taoism. I deeply believe in them. This is because I believe in the existence of deities and gods.
>
> Such things are just like that. Some of us . . . they say "Wow . . . you are Chinese. Why do you *bai* to *ang moh* [red-haired, Caucasian] god? I think, just like I mentioned, more than ten years ago, he [Nezha] came before me . . . I believe strongly that I have a destiny with Taoism.

As for SYK, subsequent to his inappropriate behavior of 骂天 (*ma tian* or reprimanding the heavens), the bodhisattva *Guan yin* appeared before him and led him to affirm the existence of spiritual realities:

> . . . end of 1999, I remembered it was in the Gregorian calendar the month of November, the evening of the final Saturday, I dreamt of *Guan yin*. I dreamt that she came over for a while . . . then after which she disappeared. Then from then on, I began to believe that there are such things.

At the same time, as the other gods or deities in Taoism continuously revealed themselves to him, his interest in the religion grew:

> This was because I would continuously dream of 大二爷伯 *Da er ye bo* [First and Second lord or uncle] or *Tua li ah pek* [in Hokkien] . . . these deities who help to govern hell . . . 黑白无常 *hei bai wu chang* [Black and White Impermanence or hell guards]. In our Taoism, in folk religion, these deities who help to govern hell . . . hell deities . . . that is to say he "hooks" the souls of the deceased . . . the two who are very common now are called *Tua li ah pek* . . . I continuously dreamt of them. Then more and more, I got interested in the religion of Taoism.

He also highlighted his various approaches to test the existence of these deities and found them to be real:

> I cannot say they do not exist because I have tested them. I have used many methods to test . . . drawing of lots, asking the deities, everything I have used to test. Everyone [of the deities] exists. Because, some more, I am also investigating this. That is why I will go into deeper understanding. So no matter how we say it, when you go into deeper understanding, you have to test and see. In my personal opinion, you have to test and see if they exist.

Although KT did not encounter a particular god or deity in his dreams, he did dream of a Taoist temple which he subsequently visited after the dream. As a result of the visit, he began his lifelong adherence to Taoism:

> Why Taoism ah . . . ah, since younger . . . interested in Chinese culture . . . then when I am . . . after my O Levels, I have a . . . I received a calling . . . a revelation to . . . to learn more about Taoism . . . It is through a dream. So after that I went to the place that I dreamt of . . . and this is where I started to . . . to know . . . realize that there is a scripture chanting class . . . scripture chanting group . . . ya . . . in this temple. So I just started my practice there . . . to learn the scriptures and pick up the basics of Taoism.

An inexplicable divine force or power is another way the sacred beings manifested themselves to a number of the participants. Besides dreams, the adherents also described their recognition of spiritual realities as these realities manifested themselves as an inexplicable force or a form of indirect help. For JK and KSY, who are Buddhists, the force was felt as they came before a spiritual or holy monk. JK's experience, which she also attributed to destiny, was unique in that the force emitted from the monk brought her sons, sister, and herself to their knees:

JK   The reason why I took Refuge was because of the visit by a monk who has very high standards in his moral conduct. He is a foreigner . . . from Canada. So I went to see. When I saw him, I immediately knelt in front of him. So this is destiny. Before this, I have met a lot of masters but did not want to take the Refuge. At that time I thought, taking Refuge is a form of vow. So with a vow, there are many things that I cannot do. At that time, I was married and I thought I would not be able to keep the vows. So I did not take the Refuge. Until I met this holy man . . . when I saw him, I immediately knelt down. So I said I wanted to take Refuge with him. Then I brought my two sons to take Refuge with him and also my younger sister. All of them . . . when they saw him, they knelt

Emerging Domain: Recognition

before him. So this is a type of destiny. This is because . . . as we say . . . a holy man of high standing . . . he has this power.

KSY So sometimes my mum says, "After the Sunday chanting session, you want to seek blessings from the lama. He is very spiritually attained." And I actually do believe that . . . there is a certain sort of positive energy even though . . . And I believe that that is true. Like there can be a certain sort of positive energy being transferred. So . . . that's . . . I was like "Okay . . . why not?" . . . And . . . so if the lama is there, why not, right?

Both SY and JE, who are Taoists, encountered similar experiences with a divine force that attracted and drew them into the Taoist temples.

SY Then on one occasion, the teacher said that there was going to be tuition . . . then it was cancelled. Then I, since I had the time, said that I would go to the temple to take a look. When I stepped into the temple, I was drawn by the temple . . . like a magnetic force . . . . From then on, whatever I went there to ask, all were answered. Don't know . . . this kind of thing is very strange.

JE Right . . . there is a special kind of feeling. This is to say . . . at home there is no such feeling . . . when you are outside . . . you don't have this kind of feeling. When, for example, you step into the temples, I tell you . . . you are very relaxed . . . you are able to loosen up, very happy lor. Your type of happiness . . . is to say you are not able to use words to express "I am so happy." It is this kind of feeling.

Similarly for JH, he experienced the help offered by the deities when he served at the *shen tan*:

> When you experienced it or went through it . . . when you help a *shen tan*, unknown to you . . . he [god or deity] will help you behind the scene. Of course it is not in those evil things . . . not in like striking lottery. That is to say in many things, he will help you without you realizing or knowing it . . . .

The third way in which spiritual realities manifested themselves to the participants is via *gan ying* or "resonantal or symbiotic interaction of stimulus and response,"[22] a concept that is found within traditional Chinese understanding. For SL, a Buddhist, she described her interactions with Buddha as:

---

22. Chappell, "Religious Identity and Openness," 12.

> This is because I feel that there is a very strong interaction. When you have a need, you feel that there are many things you are not able to handle . . . when you reach this point . . . there will naturally be a response. So when you tell your woes to Buddha, he will help you to bring about a change in your life.

As for BD, also a Buddhist, he said that responses given by Buddha-Bodhisattva sustained his commitment to Buddhism:

> For example when we are reciting *Amitabha*, or when we are praying, we will feel something or sense something. We feel that there is a response. Maybe it is my own imagination . . . you may want to say that but I feel that there is this response. Feel that this Buddha-Bodhisattva whom I believe in—has this response. There are these responses that took place. So I became even firmer in me believing in this religion.

He also described another experience with *gan ying*—one that occurred between his teacher and himself:

> I felt that there was something wanted me to know . . . it was like someone was looking for me . . . there was someone looking for me. So naturally, inside me said "There is this feeling that someone looking for me." Then I felt very strange . . . "Who is it? Who is it?" After that I felt I was writing this word—it is "Teacher is looking for me." So I made a phone call to my teacher "Teacher, is it you looking for me?" . . . "Yes. Just now, I thought of you." So I had this kind of experience . . . Do you understand? At that time I was in meditation, I saw that I had this sense of worry in my heart. I don't know how to describe it . . . I am telling you . . . felt that there was someone looking for me. I do not know who it was. But my hand naturally wrote out the words . . . there was someone looking for me . . . it is my teacher looking for me . . . someone was looking for me. When I called, I was right . . . my teacher said "Yes . . . just now, I thought of you."

KS, a Buddhist for over fifteen years, noted humorously that for himself, the Buddha provided him with a response or revelation in terms of what to do when he sought Buddha's guidance:

> But I still will believe Buddha can helping us. They found that I am crazy you know . . . ya. That's right. Especially during bad times is no people will help you that time. So maybe you might need some . . . some people [as a response from Buddha] to just in Mandarin

Emerging Domain: Recognition

we say "to give you a revelation" ... to let you know what you are supposed to do now, you see.

Finally, KT, who is a Taoist, explained his own encounters with the sacred beings or the supernatural as:

> And in religion right, it is how you experience the supernatural ... the higher beings ... How to explain in words ... I saw God today. This kind of thing we say is a response-interaction. Response-interaction, this kind of thing is it is very hard to explain through words. So you ask me to describe how it benefits me, it benefit me ... I can feel the existence ... the type of like the energy that helps me. But I cannot write in words ... this is the *Dao* ... the *Dao* helped me today ... it is very hard to describe in words. But I can say that a practitioner who practice it, right, this experience [of stimulus-response] is strong enough to let him practice it for the rest of his life.

These experiences with *gan ying* expressed by the participants are similar with Chappell's (2005) delineation of how 天台 *tian tai* Buddhism's founder Zhiyi developed *gan ying* beyond what is the general understanding, as defined briefly above. In Zhiyi's understanding, *gan ying* is the "mysterious immanence of the BuddhaDharma itself, working undetected within the manifest spiritual efforts or 'stimuli of the devotee.'"[23] For KT, the *Dao* in Taoism is the mysterious immanence. Needless to say, *gan ying* is such a powerful and beneficial experiential encounter that it is able to sustain the participants' religious identity either as Buddhists or Taoists.

The fourth way in which spiritual realities manifested themselves to the participants is through miraculous acts. In this study, the participants who are Taoists experienced two types of miraculous acts. One of them is the accurate divination provided by the *ji tong*, or divining youths/shamans, in the temples. JH explained what he saw and heard during the fortune-telling sessions conducted by the *ji tong*:

> If you cultivate your behavior and actions ... I have witnessed before ... that divining youth he did cultivate his behavior and the god or the divinity enters into him more than 80 percent of the time. This is what I experienced and saw. Very accurate. He does not need to ask any questions. After sitting down, what this 香客 *xiang ke* [person who goes to the temple to offer incense and ask for divine directions] wants to ask ... he [the divining youth] will

---

23. Ibid., 12.

just ask him "How old are you? Where do you live?" Then he can calculate/figure out and state what that person wants to ask and needs to know.

SYK also echoed similar experiences with the divining youth's ability to reveal the unknown issues in someone's life:

> That is to say when I first went down there, when they were doing the *tiao tong*, that was when the deity possessed the body [of the divining youth] . . . he [divining youth/deity] helped me. The things that my family did not know [about me], that my friends did not know [about me], he mentioned everything. From then on, I believed even more firmly their [the deities] existence. Then from then on, I developed more and more interest in Taoism.
>
> Then after that, I introduced my camp's catering supervisor to go and ask [the divining youth]. He did not say much to me. The first time he went to ask, what happened in his home was all revealed . . . his quarrels with his wife, for whatever reasons he was quarreling with his wife, everything was revealed. They were all shocked. Whatever that were hidden in his life were uncovered. Everyone whom I introduced had all that were hidden uncovered. Because I did not know, frankly I did not know . . . I did not intentionally bring them there to have whatever that were hidden uncovered. They said they wanted to find someone . . . and . . . I introduced them to come. I did not realize that they would all say that the divining youth was very accurate. One by one they went to try . . . only then they knew. I have seen Muslims who went to ask, Christianity [Christians] who went to ask . . . there were.

The second type of miraculous act is the taste of the food that has been offered to ancestors undergoing a change in taste. Four of the Taoist participants emphatically stated that the food they brought tasted bland after being offered to their ancestors. KL said:

> Yes . . . she will [eat the food]! I believe! Because . . . I don't know what to call it . . . test it before. For example, my mother enjoys *ching tng* [a sweet cooling soup, filled with gingko nuts, white fungus, and other cooling ingredients] . . . and you know *tau suan* [sweet mung bean soup] right. Okay, there was once we came to *bai* . . . I bought one serving of *ching tng* and one serving of *tau suan* . . . so after pray . . . we will normally . . . whatever we can eat, we will eat. So we can taste . . . the taste is different. Things that have been eaten [by my mum's spirit] and things not eaten [by my mum's spirit] . . . when we take and eat . . . the taste is different.

Emerging Domain: Recognition

So I believe... I believe! Okay... this is to say... what has been touched by another world... so when you eat... it is not as fragrant. Because she has touched it... it is not as fragrant, not as sweet... there is a little smelly and sour. Whereas the *tau suan*, she did not touched it... so it is still the same... as tasty.

In a rather lengthy interaction with SW, KCL, and YN in a group interview, they helped me understand this unique phenomenon. The exchange with them went as follows:

Q   Do you think that... throughout the whole process, they eat... what they have touched... after that when you eat... that there is a difference?

SW   The taste is different.

KCL   Things that are used to *bai* ancestors... the taste is lost.

YN   After *bai*... it is like this.

KCL   All the while, it has been like this.

YN   Because... they say... when we *bai* ancestors... they suck up the taste.

Q   Have you tasted the difference?

SW   Yes. For example, *bai* the gods and *bai* the ancestors... the things taste bland... the things... after *bai* the ancestors taste bland.

Q   Can you describe in what ways is it bland? Is it formerly it was salty and now it is not salty... previously it was sweet and now it is no longer sweet... previously it was fragrant... now it is no longer fragrant?

YN   You are right. It is different.

Q   Okay... it is different and you are able to tell the difference? Have you experienced this?

ALL   Yes.

SW   When we eat it . . . it is no longer delicious.

Q   Oh . . . no longer delicious?

KCL   This is real!

KCL, YN
    After we bring it home . . . it is really no longer delicious!

SW   If you go to the Qing Ming Festival, if you go to the grave there and *bai* . . . it is more strenuous . . . all the things no longer delicious.

KCL   The taste . . . there is no longer any taste.

Q   It is not because you left it there . . . outside . . . for a period of time?

ALL   No, no, no!

Q   It is because the ancestors suck up the taste?

SW   Yes.

Q   So does this . . . spur you on to give them food to eat because they really eat?

KCL, YN
    Got . . . according to this reason . . . it does.

Q   So this becomes a form of motivation . . . an encouragement . . . a type of strength? Do all of you think it is this way?

ALL   Yes!

    To further follow up on this phenomenon, I also spoke with KC. She pointed out that there are various "logical explanations" (e.g., leaving the food out for too long, chemical changes within the food) offered for this phenomenon, but she also acknowledged that these explanations do not fully account for why the food offered to the gods or deities does not undergo a change in taste and only those offered to ancestors do. Kuah-Pearce also recorded this phenomenon in her research and noted that, "the food offered to the hungry ghosts [or ancestors] tastes "flat" and funny, unlike that offered to the deities."[24] It is no wonder that these miraculous acts have an obvious impact on these four participants—in encouraging and motivating them to continue to offer food to their ancestors for the rest of their lives.

Discussion

All the participants acknowledged that over the course of their lives, they came to recognize the enfolding presence and power of spiritual realities existing within Buddhism and Taoism. Their recognition of the presence of spiritual realities began via participating alongside family members or friends in rituals or practices within their social environments. Even though the roles of family and friends are important, it is critical to point out they are channels that facilitated the participants to come face-to-face with the presence and power of these realities embedded within the religions. As a result of recognizing spiritual realities, the participants attested that they knew where to go and to whom they should turn for help during personal crises.

While the participation subdomain revealed that the participants were the initiators of the interactions with spiritual realities, the revelation subdomain demonstrated a different process. Through revelations, the spiritual realities, particularly the sacred beings or forces, revealed themselves and initiated the interactions with the participants. The mysterious nature of these realities also meant that the participants, Buddhists or Taoists, had different experiences with a variety of revelations—be it destiny or the different forms of manifestations. As a result, recognition via revelation strongly undergirds their religious identity either as Buddhists or Taoists.

Religious identity, as defined in this study, entails an individual's awareness of and commitment to (a) a continuous and invigorating inner well-being, and (b) a sense of belonging and need to extend the well-being to the sociocultural community associated with the divine. This awareness and commitment arises out of an individual's reciprocal interactions with the divine and the sociocultural community associated with the divine. The recognition domain reveals that these facets are evident in the experiences of the participants. Not only did the participants interact with and come to recognize spiritual realities via being coparticipants in their sociocultural communities, more significantly these realities also interacted in distinct

24. Kuah-Pearce, *State, Society and Religious Engineering*, 70.

ways with them. Thus, the recognition domain in which the participants immersed themselves revealed to them the presence and power of spiritual realities. This domain provides a useful and unique perspective into how the religious identity of Chinese Singaporeans who are Buddhists or Taoists is primarily established and subsequently sustained by the dimensions of spiritual realities.

In the next chapter, another domain will be explored—appreciation. This domain will shed further insights into the participants' continued experiences of wholeness, rejuvenation, and stability brought about by the power and presence of spiritual realities. As a result of these positive experiences, the participants expressed their appreciation toward these realities. At the same time, the participants' disagreements vis-à-vis the Christians' responses toward these spiritual realities will be discussed, particularly in light of how these negative sentiments served to strengthen the participants' appreciation of these realities inherent in Buddhism and Taoists.

Chapter 6

Emerging Domain: Appreciation

The previous discussion on the recognition domain revealed that as the participants came to recognize the presence and power of spiritual realities through participation and revelation, their religious identity came to be established and sustained. As they participated in the practices and rituals that introduced and attuned them to the presence and power of these realities over the years, the participants knew whom they can turn to and what they could do in times of difficulty. Following their appeals to these realities for help, the realities in turn revealed their power in distinct ways in order to aid the participants.

Having overcome the difficult times with the help rendered by these realities, the participants developed an ongoing and deep sense of gratitude. In particular, they were appreciative of how the spiritual realities brought about transformation, direction, and protection. During the interviews, I was surprised by the openness of many of the participants as they shared about their or their family members' difficult moments in life, and how the spiritual realities provided either the necessary transformation, direction, or protection such that they were able to surmount those difficult times. As a result, I caught a glimpse into how the appreciation domain functioned in their lives to establish and sustain their religious identity.

For many of the participants, the transformation and direction came about as they sought the help of spiritual realities through engaging in the sacred acts—i.e., practices and rituals, as well as with the sacred texts of *suttas* or the *Dao de jing*. Amidst the periods of need and crises experienced by the participants, these acts and texts brought about spiritual strength and insights that enabled them to cope with the present realities in light of future realities. As a result, the participants were deeply grateful for the spiritual assistance rendered.

The physical protection given by spiritual realities to the participants also contributed to their appreciation. Through the use of practices and rituals, either self-performed or conducted by the divining youth, the participants and their family members were kept from physical harm or disturbances by an evil spirit. As a gesture of their gratitude, the participants made offerings to the gods or deities who rendered the protection.

The data also revealed how the participants' appreciation of the presence and power of spiritual realities within Buddhism and Taoism is strengthened by their disagreement with the responses of Christians they have encountered toward these realities—such as the criticisms of the gods and deities and the disrespectful manner in treating the home altars for the ancestors. At the same time, they also expressed their disagreement with the spiritual realities articulated by Christians—i.e., what they heard being taught in churches or presented during evangelism did not cohere with their experiences. Thus, not surprisingly, the expression of their disagreement during the interviews also included sentiments of unhappiness, repulsion, and skepticism. For the participants who had these experiences, they had been going to church for a number of years or visited churches a number of times. In light of their negative experiences with Christians, many of the participants were rather surprised that a Christian was interested in researching more about Buddhists and Taoists in Singapore.

Thus, prior to the interviews, the participants often asked me to explain the purpose of my study. Having explained to them about the nature of my study and my intention to learn from their experiences, many of them expressed that my research would help other religious adherents in Singapore gain a deeper understanding of Buddhism and Taoism in Singapore. A number of them also agreed that such an understanding would benefit interreligious relationships in Singapore. Thus, they were candid and open with me about their past experiences with other Christians. Their perspectives enriched my data collection as I emerged from these interviews with deeper insights about how disagreement reinforced the appreciation domain.

Emerging Domain: Appreciation

Appreciation of the Enfolding Presence and Power of Spiritual Realities

Transformation

The transformation experienced by the participants, as described by them, is marked by terms such as "joy," "awoke," "being enlightened," "fulfillment," "happier every day," and "well-being." These words and phrases emerged as a result of the participants engaging in the practices that provided a channel to access the help readily rendered by spiritual realities—such as meditation, 念佛绕佛 *nian fo rao fo,* which is chanting while circumambulating the statue of Buddha,[1] and gleaning insights from the teachings.

Overcoming Personal Crises

For most of the participants, they experienced the impact of transformation over the course of their lives. For PC, JK, and AS, who had to cope with unexpected deaths of family members, divorce, and depression respectively, they recounted at length how their transformation brought about by spiritual realities—e.g., insights into the impermanence of all physical entities and chanting the *suttas*—helped them overcome their personal crises:

PC   Yes, actually it is . . . when . . . my third sister passed away after complications after her delivery. She had . . . she delivered smoothly but then the second day she fell from the hospital bed and then just passed away because there is . . . the blood clot that was found in her lungs. So it really caught me by surprise . . . it is like shock, more shock. It is like . . . things is like so unpredictable, it is like you take things for granted, it is like you didn't know that . . . you think that everything is so smooth and how come suddenly this kind of bad things happen. It is like struck me that things are impermanent. And then another incident is when my father-in-law died, I mean he had a stroke for many years. So when he passed away in my house and we call the person to come and take him away—the body. He was strapped up in a mat . . . it is like . . . it also struck me it is like when we die, it is just like a rubbish . . . being wrapped up and just disposed like that. I also don't know how I coped. It is only until now that I learn more about Buddhism

---

1. Mitchell, *Buddhism*, 188. While making the rounds, Buddhists will hold prayer beads, moving each bead at a time with a finger while reciting prayers and incantations of Buddhas, bodisattvas, and deities.

then I try to link it back . . . it is like to help me get over it now . . . because even over the years, I miss my sis and I will cry. It is like . . . I felt like it is a . . . depression and that kind of thing. So but now when I learn more about this thing [impermanence] . . . more about Buddhism, I don't cry that often . . .

JK During 1994 and 1995 . . . my marriage life was unhappy . . . that is one reason. So I was thinking, why is life like that? Surely, there must be a reason. Thus, I must go and look for a path to walk. I wanted to know why it is like that. Moreover if I have a support for my emotional needs, I will be happier . . . I need to look for a philosophy, a religion to solve the basic problems in how I think. Or why is my life . . . like that—something that can give answers to these problems. What is more important is . . . that I am able to find myself . . . to find my true self . . . what am I, an individual, really made up of. This is because Buddha said that our Five Senses are affected by our *karma* from our previous life. So in this life, when you know what is cause and effect, you will find that what you say, how you act, your intentions . . . all these are affected by previous karma or the present karma that will affect the future . . . it really changed my perspective toward life. Moreover, I feel that besides this religion, there is no other religion can replace this religion in this world.

AS I was emotionally scarred. Later on, when I was twenty-seven to twenty-nine years old, I felt I was abnormal . . . had depression. If I had continued on, no one was able to help me. There was only one road for me—to take my own life. I experienced a few obstacles in my life . . . I could not continue to spiral downwards in this manner. I would chant *suttas*, go to the monasteries to chant *suttas* . . . the Ksitigarbha *sutta* . . . it is for removal of bad karma. Then I would just chant for a short while and then I would leave. Then when I was thirty-eight to forty years old, I would go look for the library and then look for the whole *sutta* and then read it at home . . . chant it through once. If I don't know how, then I would go to the monastery to chant for some time before going home. That was where I started . . . I began to understand more . . . I also chanted the *sutta* . . . for filial piety and so naturally later on, at about forty years old, naturally my heart of compassion arose. When my heart of compassion arose, I stopped taking meat . . . stopped eating meat and slowly I grew calmer and closer to Buddhism. From then till now, from forty to fifty, I saw that I improved every year. Year after year... last time I do not recite *Amitabha* daily but now I do it daily... recite *Amitabha*, copy the *suttas* and recite *Amitabha*.

For JK, who experienced an unhappy marriage and divorce, her profound transformation brought about by Buddhism filled her with joy and gratitude:

> I am very happy in this religion... I have received the greatest joy in my life... my destiny is with Buddhism... this will not change. If someone asks me to believe in Christ or other religions, I will chase him or her away.

As for AS, his transformation led him to forgive his father's abuse toward him as a child:

> My father's attitude was very bad. However, over time, I am actually grateful toward him. There is no longer hate. In the beginning, I hated him, before I came into contact with Dharma, I hated him. I did not do anything wrong... he hit and scold without any reasons... no need for any reasons. When I did right, you scolded. When I did wrong, you also scolded and hit. So my attitude became abnormal. Later I came into contact with the Dharma. So for these grievances and hate, I felt that I could let them go. Let them go and change and transform. I am grateful to them... grateful to my father and family. I was grateful to him—i.e., for giving me a chance to come into contact with something so good. Now there is no longer hate.

Renewing Negative Attitudes

Another form of transformation overwhelmingly experienced by the participants is in their responses to people around them and various situations in life. The participants also informed me that their friends or family members affirmed these transformed responses. For a number of the participants, their attitude displayed joyfulness or happiness:

> AS I am satisfied inwardly, fulfilled... that is good enough for me... inwardly rich—that is good enough. It is being rich spiritually... it is very difficult to describe. Sometimes, there is this happiness... this feeling of joyfulness... joy that flows out from inside. In Buddhism, there is this happiness...Last time when I was serving in the army, during my reservist time... I have to go yearly... so when I changed every year... I was not aware. But toward

the latter part, they [fellow reservists] told me "You changed a lot." There are changes. It was no longer cursing the moment I reported for reservist . . . scold the government, scold the military camp for wasting my time . . . toward the latter part, I mellowed down—my temper, attitude, actions, especially my temper—face that was always angry. Last time, I looked like a hooligan. Now I am much calmer and have mellowed down.

SL   It is because it [Buddhism] has allowed me to be happy both physically and spiritually. My physical and spirit are both quite happy. You feel that your whole . . . after repentance, the entire condition of your spirit and your thinking are transformed . . . Repentance is . . . like you did something wrong and you repent before Buddha . . . so that daily we will remember what wrongs have we done . . . so that it is necessary to change . . . must change. Another aspect is that I am also happy myself. I am happier. Last time, I was always worried. But now I am laughing daily. So people used to say . . . "If you worry, a day will pass by. If you laugh, a day will also pass by. So why do you choose to worry? Why do you not choose to laugh?" Last time, I did not understand the meaning of this.

MA   Ya . . . because Buddhism also . . . asks us not to be attached to anything . . . nonattachment . . . because everything is impermanent and there is a nonenduring entity. So it has made me happier in a sense that I try not to look at things so seriously. I mean even if . . . criticisms, or those praise, or promotions . . . you know . . . ya. In a sense . . . more detached . . . that is why happier. I am happier . . . ya.

For CW and BT, they were able to lessen their bad- or quick-tempered nature. As a result of reflecting on scriptural tenets and engaging in the practices, they are calmer and more restrained in responding to situations around them:

CW   Well . . . being able to keep calm as I was quite bad-tempered, quick-tempered . . . ya. So through the learning, reflecting, and practicing of Buddhism . . . I am able to look at things differently. That means I wouldn't react to situations that make me angry, as like in the past. That means I am able to react differently and view things differently also.

BT   Oh . . . over these last two years, I have met with some issues . . . . When faced with these issues, you may feel very infuriated. So

Emerging Domain: Appreciation

infuriated that, my personality used to be . . . I have an explosive temper . . . but will practice patience and endurance . . . . So have learnt patience and endurance . . . Buddhism is talking about cause and effect . . . talking about karma. So, in this incident, it happened in my home . . . I moved into this new home for more than two-years . . . a resale place . . . I ran into a few loan sharks. But this home . . . targeted by the loan sharks . . . so they came to spray paint and etc. . . . it made me . . . I became really infuriated . . . very angry, right or not? Your whole person . . . is affected by what has happened. You are really angry . . . very angry. So, perhaps from this, it is like . . . since for me . . . this religion has taught about what is known has cause and effect, so usually Buddhists deeply believe in cause and effect. So, because I know the process of how it happened, let's say for example if we had an attitude of taking revenge, then of course since hate and revenge begets hate and revenge . . . when will it all end? If I . . . I during that time did not use what I learnt to restrain my kind of actions, So at least my behavior did not turn violent . . . that kind attitude did not come forth. So it has become forbearance and long-suffering.

Besides the transformation of bad or negative attitudes, a number of the participants experienced the transformation of their minds through meditation—which led to better health, calmer disposition, and less greed for material things. CH and MA reflected how the process helped them:

CH   Oh ya . . . ok. Why I continue because my health was no good and when I went for the retreat, I find it very peaceful and calm . . . peaceful and calm and that is how I find that the meditation helped me a lot. It helped me a lot. And of course, if you go to learn more about meditation, you find that it helps to clear your mind . . . it will affect your physical body. You know, you are actually training your mind and you actually feel very peaceful and calm.

MA   I think meditation is very important. I think that is the gift of the teaching. So . . . I think when you are very calm, you are very so-called . . . your mind is very clear, you tend to understand the teaching better. The teachings actually sort of get into you. Then from there you actually slowly day by day you actually improve. Ya . . . you really know . . . so far from the day . . . I started until now is like . . . I am less anger . . . less angry, less greedy and . . . you are really . . . you actually in fact getting happier every day.

Direction

It is worth noting that in addition to being appreciative of the transformation experienced, many of the participants also expressed their appreciation toward the sacred texts in Buddhism and Taoism. According to them, these texts and insights are "practical," "holistic," "logical," and "helpful," and thus they became a stable niche of values that provided the direction for them to live right in this life in preparation for the next life. Thus, it is no surprise that these sacred teachings also played a role in the transformation the participants experienced, as discussed in the previous section.

A number of the Buddhist participants highlighted the importance of engaging in these texts over participation in rituals such as 法会 *fa hui*, or dharma purification rituals, as these rituals are deemed to be superstitious. Thus, they adhere to Buddha's exhortation to investigate and practice the teachings in order to discover which ones are helpful in providing direction for life instead of unquestioning obedience to these teachings. In general, the teachings provide direction for the participants through two different ways: insights and ethics.

Insights

Insights primarily refer to the understanding the participants gleaned from the teachings that pertain to realities beyond what is observable in the physical world. For JK, she is appreciative of the Vajrayana doctrines for what these teachings can reveal in terms of who she is and how the universe is constructed:

> ... when you enter the Emptiness, all the whole world and the whole universe ... the whole Milky Way ... the whole solar system and universe ... it is all equal. So see how it is different. So that is why we are looking for Vajrayana ... the highest goal is to reach you find out yourself ... When you find out yourself, you try to practice Emptiness. If you can go into Rigpa, you already find out yourself. You find yourself means you find another things in your body. And these things are very very important. Once you reach this one, you will know the whole world ... how they construct. You have every sense.

Emerging Domain: Appreciation

As for JL, the notions of impermanence or emptiness deeply influenced him in terms of how he views surrounding realities and conducts himself:

> Like I mean sufferings and impermanence and of course the way they view life and everything.... I think maybe in terms of... in regard to some... maybe some event in life... like maybe you are going through work and then you say that "Ok... the society is like full of money and greed and so on and so forth..." and then you start to think that "Eh... maybe this is... there are some thing more than that to life...."
>
> And ultimately, I think there is one... which is the notion of Emptiness... because... we tend to take ourselves very seriously as this one is our own identity... right. But in fact, if you really break it down right, we are only made up of atoms, molecules and even you break them down into quarks... or gluons now.... Gluons... I mean even smaller than the atom, ya. So... it is very refreshing idea and its also, I mean so far science has told us ... that its... we... we are unable to really pinpoint where is the so-called consciousness, where is the self... ya. So I think this is quite interesting idea. Ya... because the teaching of Buddhism also ... also asks us not to be attached to anything... nonattachment ... because everything is impermanent and there is a nonenduring entity. So it has made me happier in a sense that I try not to look at things so seriously. I mean even if... criticisms, or those praise, or promotions... you know... ya. In a sense... more detached ... that is why happier. I am happier... ya.

In CW's opinion, his appreciation of the Buddhist *suttas* came about because of the *suttas*' consistency with science, thereby providing him with insights into realms beyond what he could see and the motivation to gain more insights. He notes:

> ... it is very consistent with science. So therefore... as seekers of the truth, we would continue to practice Buddhism. And hopefully, we can realize even more insights. Well... if you talk about the Big Bang theory... you know... it is already captured in the *suttas*... ya. And if you talk about the theory of evolution ... we... the human race evolved through time as well. And when we talk about quantum physics, there is a theory of multiverse... And to... to Buddhists, we can coexist within a certain time and space as well. And we might not even see it. For example, the ghost realm... you know there could be other beings in this room even though physically only two of us are here... so there is

a coexistence of other beings in different time and space. And then science also talks about multidimensional world.

Similarly for JE, what she discovered in the Taoist scriptures gives her understanding into the future in terms of where she will go after death. As a result, this provides her with a sense of security as well as a basis to teach morals to her son:

> For Taoism, I think sometimes . . . my own thoughts . . . during this time, it has been rather good. It does help me . . . help some of what you hope for . . . you will have something to look forward to. Then I like it because . . . if not next time after I die, I don't know where I will go. At least there is a place to go to. It is better than if you wander around . . . don't know where to go. I don't know how next time will be . . . but at least while on earth, you will see those scriptures . . . ok . . . how are they like . . . then you will say . . . at least after you die, there is something to look forward to . . . that is to say you can go to this place.
>
> In Taoism, we have houses. Taoism mirrors our life in reality now . . . we have cars, airplanes . . . did you see when we do merits . . . we have airplanes and cars . . . got whatever. Then in Taoism, we talk about eighteen levels of hell. Now I keep reminding my son of this . . . telling him "You cannot do bad things, you cannot tell lies."

Ethics

The often-repeated phrase that many of the participants used when describing the teachings of both religions is "it is a form of education philosophy"—i.e., these texts provide ethical guidelines for the participants to 做人 *zuo ren*, or be a human. *Zuo ren*, a long-treasured Chinese value, primarily encompasses the ways of conducting oneself appropriately (e.g., humble, caring) and uprightly (e.g., not deceitful and devious) regardless of whether one is alone or before others.

According to KS and CK, one of the helpful principles derived from Buddhist *suttas* is "to know yourself." According to them, in gaining self-awareness, they engage in the right actions and are aware of the directions to take as they move through life:

> KS . . . because for Buddhism more important, they got one point . . . for what this Buddha to say that "You must know yourself." Because for know yourself . . . this thing . . . I found is very important

> ... That's why you must know yourself. I found this word is very practical for the modern ... modern life. A lot of people doesn't know themselves ... don't know what to do ... don't know where they come from ... don't know which direction to go. That's why I believe is more important on that you [know yourself] .... Because you know yourself, know yourself how to do.

CK Okay. Because the most important is to find meaning in life. That you are able to say ... Why are we here, what is your purpose ... you know ... If you don't have this direction or compass, you will just go on with life just doing this or doing that ... there is no alternative to life ... that is not far-sighted. Of course you know Buddha's teaching is about rebirth ... you know ... things like that. The whole thing ... an ecosystem. Most important thing is karma ... karma means the action. What you do ... you know you have to answer for it.

For BT, CW, and YT, Buddhist teachings constantly provide a framework for right behavior, especially in relating or responding to others. BT noted:

> It is a form of education ... an education. What did I learn? It is ... the most important according to them ... is how your action ... that is your personal behavior ... behavior. So, what I learnt in these five years, what I learnt ... for a person ... we need to talk about our own behavior. Behaviors follow who we are—for example good or evil. What you do or how you act can bring about a negative consequence ... it is demonstrated through our actions. So in these five years, what I learnt ... the most important point is ... for me is ... is actions ... how we act.
>
> Buddhism ... because it allows you personally to read the *suttas* and then reflect about them. As for what the monks teach about some of the Dharma, you can go deeper and then ponder about them ... to reflect on them. After that, from your reflections, you think about ... what you did recently or in the past ... the things that you did ... what has happened ... from these reflections ... you can explore ... If you are not a Buddhist, maybe this thing will not turn out this way. Maybe it will be worse ... of course with some Dharma, it will help us to restrain ourselves from doing something which we should not be doing. Or it helps us to do something better.

As for CW, he stated:

> But the taking of the Five . . . the Three Refuge and practicing the Five Precepts mindfully . . . those are more important. And then of course when you go after that is to give compassion . . . lovingkindness . . . sorry. . . loving kindness to others . . . in Buddhist term is called *Metta*. Radiate the lovingkindness to others . . . then realize the impermanence . . . I don't go drinking alcohol anymore after I have taken the Buddhist path. So it is just like . . . I am not drinking with them [colleagues] . . . So it is like not participating . . . Socially I am still around but I don't drink with them anymore.

Finally, for YT, Buddhist teachings helped him to respond with lovingkindness to his daughter during a particular Chinese New Year celebration:

> So by practicing all these things . . . understanding each other and . . . lovingkindness especially, I think, there was one case that I can start is that . . . on the first day of Chinese New Year. My daughter suddenly . . . somehow she had some emotional ups and down and then she started to cry for no reason . . . So, if I wasn't practicing Buddhism, probably I will shout at her or even punish her or beat her up and all these. But then, I start to look . . . see things from a different perspective . . . "Hey, why is she behaving this way? Might something that causes her to do this." So, what I did was that I just give her a hug and tell her that everything is okay . . . you know. So by consoling her and by showing her lovingkindness, somehow, her attitude starts to change. So before that I would use violence against violence . . . so when she misbehaves, you just have to stop her . . . basically fighting fire with fire, you know. So we realize that is not the case. And understanding how to apply the Buddha teaching in this . . . understanding her and seeing that she is in suffering right now, what I need to give her is basically lovingkindness . . . right. . . and then we talk about things later. First of all, make her feel comfortable . . . make her feel loved. And once she is comfortable . . . she is calmed down, and then everything will be okay.

Similarly for KT and LX, Taoist teachings taught them to "stay low" or be humble and serve all people regardless of being treated well or badly. Quoting from a chapter in the *Dao de jing*, which uses water as an analogy, both of them described the lessons they learned:

> KT One of the ideas is to . . . like the benefits of water . . . to stay low. Not to like . . . try to impress people and do things that . . . to show off or what. So I always believe in doing good to others but always just have the . . . that is the main objective is to do good . . . but do

not go and like just do for the sake of showing people that I am doing something. So this really guides me along in what I do . . . so I do not need to seek all those recognition, or I don't even seek all those people . . . like knowing it's me . . . like I am the person who is doing all these. I believe that people will know who is doing it . . . . Just do my best and that's it . . . to serve my best.

LX   "The highest excellence is like that of water . . ." . . . water . . . it benefits everybody . . . be it benefit the plant, be it benefit the water that we are drinking or whatever. But it never once thought of receiving any repayment. And regardless of whether you throw good or bad things into the ocean, they still absorb. They still accept. They never say they reject anything but they still benefit the people . . . ya . . . benefit everything. This is what sometimes some . . . this kind of philosophy that keep us going on. Like maybe some of the time in our life . . . maybe we will have mistakes . . . such things. So we will try to . . . you know . . . think of this kind of philosophy to keep us going on.

The participants' appreciation of the sacred texts or teachings—in providing life's direction by shedding spiritual insights concerning present and future realities and the ethical principles for daily living—cannot be overstated. This is because as a sacred or divine frame of reference, the teachings provide answers for the "why of existence"[2] as well as guidelines to live harmoniously with fellow humans. At the same time, the participants also expressed their appreciation toward the noncoercive manner in terms of how Buddhist *suttas* and Taoists scriptures are taught.

For PC and NY, who are both Buddhists, they pointed out that Buddha never forced his teachings upon his followers:

PC   Buddha never insists that you have to believe everything he says. You should practice it to see whether is it true or not that kind of thing. So it doesn't insist that you . . . he wants you to practice and witness it yourself. Then you believe it. Don't believe everything what he says or what his disciples say. So this is the thing I like it . . . . is like it is more truthful in a sense. It doesn't impose a kind of forceful belief in that "Trust me and you will go where . . ." that kind of thing. If you don't trust me, you will have . . . you will suffer that kind of consequences . . . that kind.

---

2. Kohn and Roth, "Introduction," 4.

NY   We . . . we don't just accept things that forced . . . forced upon you. It is very much of . . . you know . . . that you really investigate yourself. Unlike other forms . . . other religions. Other religions . . . where they come to you and they try to convert you or impose their views on you . . . Buddhism is a little more open-ended . . . .

As for KT, who is a Taoist, his at-length description of how Taoism transmits its teachings through the rituals was insightful:

> Taoism . . . we do not have any mass or sermons . . . that means the priest do not go and talk and tell a congregation in a classroom setting. So usually we will preach through a ritual . . . that means from a ritual right, we reenact certain values to the people. Like how the priest portray and show respect to the deities right, he is also reflect on the people how they should show respect to their ancestors and to their parents. This is a form of respect. So through rituals, that is why you see Taoist rituals are very colorful. So we use rituals as a form to teach them . . . to teach the people . . . like how to . . . when we do the ceremony to free the spirits from suffering or what. They will do certain rituals. But these rituals . . . these enactments right, these . . . the performance of these rituals, it have half a meaning of like explaining to a person how we should live life . . . certain values. So we use the rituals to teach the people. So ritual, to us, is a very important aspect. You cannot say that in Taoism . . . you just study and do not practice it. Ya, of course the prostration itself, it teaches a person how to be good, how to lie low, how to stay low and sometimes to stand and also to respect . . . to show respect to our elders. So all these values are taught through the rituals . . . how we stand, how we hold our hands together. Like when we hold our hands together, cupping our hands right, it symbolize the 太极 *taiji* [the Great Ultimate, which is a balance of *Yin* and *Yang*] symbol. So as we hold, we also talk about how we embrace differences . . . how we learn. So all these values is through the rituals . . . they teach the followers.

Protection

The discussion in the above sections reveals that the transformation experienced and the direction received by the participants are primarily internal in nature (i.e., attitudes, mind). The protection they received from spiritual realities, as revealed in the data, is both physical as well as internal. Through specific petitions to the gods and deities for help, and the performance of rituals, the participants experienced different forms of protection.

Daily Protection

For JE, through the daily ritual of *bai bai* and the occasional specific visits to the temples to seek the help of the deities or gods, she found refuge, sustenance, and an inherent sense of peace that protected her during difficult times:

> It is a type of ... how do you say ... is type of refuge and sustenance ... I think it is a form of refuge and sustenance. Refuge and sustenance is like ... to say ... there are some things which cannot be resolved or to say ... that is ... equivalent to ... there is some hope ... for example when ... there is no way matters can be resolved or say I need ... there are some things ... some things ... there is no way to go and do them ... so have to depend on own strength to ... move forward. Strength ... is like protection, there are some things which are impossible for us ... okay, for example, this incident happens to me now ... even with my human strength ... there is no way around ... so I need the spirit ... a type of strength to propel me forward. Some of them ... like for example when I have difficulties, I can go and *bai* to *Da bo gong* ... When you *bai* ... there is protection. There is a ... when you *bai* ... you will feel more peaceful inside. When you offer the incense, you will feel more at peace within yourself. Then the entire day ... you will be happy. You will ... it is like there is something protecting you.

SW, KCL, and YN echoed similar sentiments when expressing that they always *bai bai* for peace and protection at the efficacious Guan yin Temple every time they shop at Bugis Junction (a large mall in central Singapore):

> So for example, when we go to Bugis to walk [around], then we will go there [Guan yin Temple] ... Just burn joss sticks ... *bai bai* ... Oh ... we say ... since we are there, since we are near Guan yin Temple, we just burn joss sticks, *bai bai* ... ask for protection and peace. Ask for protection and peace ... when we are there ...

This is especially important for KCL, whose husband works as a driver:

Ask for peace and protection. Like for my husband . . . he needs to go for his work . . . so in the morning . . . will burn the incense before going to work and in the evening, after coming home from work . . . burn the incense again. That what he does. Going out from home . . . must be safe and sound . . . driving vehicle . . . to go for work.

Likewise, for LX and MQ, the daily *bai bai* is important to bring about safety for family members and work:

LX   So, burn joss sticks, pray . . . family safety for my family, then work will be smooth, then I will go out. That is a very basic thing that I would do everyday.

MQ   Burning joss sticks . . . it is like that. You are like . . . you want to say something to the gods . . . like you *bai* to the Great Sovereign Emperor [*Tian gong*] . . . to protect you . . . that you will be safe . . . protect you . . . that your body will be healthy . . . or that your business will be smooth-sailing . . . it is like this . . .

Special Protection

Another form of protection, one that is called upon in times of emergency, is against physical harm. One of the most interesting examples was provided by SYK, where he recounted the driving out of a malevolent or "dirty" spirit that plagued his niece for a period of time until a divining youth came to her aid by invoking the divine help offered by Taoist gods through a series of rituals:

Then she [my sister's mother-in-law] brought the child [my niece] . . . to view [house for the purpose of finding out if the house is "dirty" or "clean"]. After viewing, then continuously at night during a specific time, she will cry and say that outside of my house, there is someone. Because my mother was taking care of the child. So the thing followed [my niece] to my house. But he or she cannot enter my home because there are things [gods, deities, talismans] in my house. My house has those *bai shen* things around. He or she just stayed at the front door of my house. At night, once it was twelve, one, or two, she will cry and say that outside the window and door, there was someone watching her . . . for over a month. At last, I looked for the divining youth at my temple to come and cast a charm. That time was not consultation period . . . that is to

Emerging Domain: Appreciation

say because my case was urgent, that is why I went to them. On the day they did the rites, the next day they taught us how to do it, and after that next day, everything was solved . . .100 percent solved . . . that is to say the dirty thing which was outside followed him away. For over a month, it was more than a month.

Another example is the occasion when Taoist gods and deities ensured that the major surgery of JH's father was carried out successfully. Similarly, JE also witnessed the physical protection offered by the deities for her sister when she *bai bai*, noting that engaging *bai bai* is not an option during difficult times:

And then when I would like my husband's work to be smooth sailing, I will go and *bai bai* . . . just like this. For example, at home, when things aren't going the ways you expect, you long for this . . . you will long and go and . . . like in my family . . . when things happened to my sister, when she was sick, we hope . . . then we will go [ask] protection. Although visits to the doctor are non-negotiable, but to the gods, you must also *bai*.

As a result of the help rendered by the gods, SYK, JH, and JE made offerings to the gods in order to demonstrate their gratitude.

Through various ways, all the participants experienced transformation, direction, and protection rendered by the presence and power of spiritual realities that surround them. Transformation enabled the participants to experience wholeness through overcoming depression and suicidal thoughts, while also experiencing renewal in their minds, health, and attitudes toward others. The realities also generated insights and ethics that serve to direct the participants in terms of how to live right in the present in light of future realities. At the same time, other participants have experienced the protection of spiritual realities, both in terms of daily safety as well as during difficult times.

Appreciation via Disagreement

As pointed out earlier, the participants' appreciation of transformation, direction, and protection rendered by the presence and power of spiritual realities inherent within Buddhism and Taoism is also deepened by their disagreement with how Christians in Singapore (a) responded toward these realities and (b) expressed the teachings that are recorded in the Bible. The emergence of this facet came as a surprise to me as I did not expect that they would reveal their disagreement with Christians to a Christian researcher. Yet, to their credit, they were willing to share their encounters and insights without being disparaging toward Christianity.

Insensitivity

One of the most significant threads that emerged is the insensitive attitude adopted by Christians in responding to the spiritual realities highly regarded by Buddhists and Taoists. This insensitivity is manifested in a number of ways. One of them was the mockery of Taoism and Buddhism. For example, in LX's experience, a few of the churches in Singapore referred to the *jing shen* (literally *pure bodies*) or images of Taoist gods and deities as pieces of wood:

> Ya . . . seriously, no offense but just an open opinion . . . just like previously . . . last year or the year before, those churches, they . . . said we Taoism, we Chinese *bai* to wood . . . that kind of thing. I find that, regardless of whether religion or not religion, I feel that respect each other is a very basic thing we learn life, right? I respect you, you respect me. I feel that there is no need that you, for the sake of keeping your members or whatever reasons it is, you went to criticize other people. I find that it is not a very good thing . . .

As for SY, during his stay in a Methodist church for over three years before returning to Taoism, he also encountered similar experiences:

> So . . . ya . . . but then again, there are ways when I was there [in the church], people that I heard talking about . . . mock about Taoism and stuff like that . . . If you [a Christian] born to one side [as a Chinese], and they [Christians] are criticizing on the other side, you [a Christian] are even worse than if you are standing on just one side.

While he did not want to provide details of what the Christians said, he used three sets of 成语 *cheng yu*, or four-character Chinese sayings or idioms, to describe the Chinese Christians who criticizes Taoism. These idioms are (a) 背信弃义 *bei xin qi yi* (to turn your back on what has been entrusted to you and abandon doing righteous actions), (b) 不忠不孝 *bu zhong bu xiao* (to be disloyal and unfilial), and (c) 不仁不义 *bu ren bu yi* (neither benevolent nor righteous). He went on to point out that in criticizing Taoism, "What advantage would you [i.e., Christians] have? You have

Emerging Domain: Appreciation

nothing." In KC's experiences, she pointed out that often the mockery turns into condemnation:

> Ya . . . that is not giving due respect to other religion. Christians are usually in this manner because other religions they will respect others. But Christians will not . . . they will condemn . . . they will always say that theirs is the best and there is only one God. They will not respect other people's religion.

Another form of insensitivity highlighted by the participants is the approaches used by Christians in evangelism. For JL, he noted that "perhaps the lack of respect . . . when you tell them [Christians] that 'No, you are not interested.' But they still continue pushing you . . . ." Similarly for KC, whose children are Christians, pointed out that being overbearing creates tensions and serves no purpose:

> I would say that . . . where religion is concerned, you [Christians] should give respect to the other person. Let it be . . . and not to overdo it. When you overdo things, it becomes ugly. Yes . . . of course you can share but it must to a certain limit you don't overdo it. So when you overdo, it is as though you are forcing a person. But when this person is not ready to accept this religion, then I see that it serves no purpose.

For ET and JH, they expressed their disapproval of Christians' attempts to "pull people and come in" to churches:

ET Under what conditions you can preach about your religion? This is a very good question. To knock on doors? To send out flyers? I feel it shouldn't be like that. For a religion's revival . . . no need to do these things . . . adherents will naturally come, right?

JH Usually I tell them [Christians] . . . to each his or her own way. What you cultivate . . . in fact on God . . . what you teach in the Bible . . . I think that we are all the same. For many things, when we talk about it . . . it is to do well in the basics. We must cultivate our behavior well . . . and not discriminate other people's religion. But personally I have experienced . . . have met . . . I also do not want to discriminate people belonging to other religions. They have tried and said "Eh . . . you come over to our side." I think this is very wrong. We do not simply . . . that is to say we must respect other people's religion. We cannot simply . . . that is to pull people to come in [into our religion]. This is very inappropriate.

The final demonstration of insensitivity is what the participants view as disrespectful in the ways Christian pastors or leaders dispose of, or burn, the altars set up for ancestors and gods, and destroy the images of gods and deities when a Taoist becomes a Christian. For example, KCL recounted her repulsion toward a Christian pastor who burnt the altars of the ancestors and gods after her friend became a Christian. As a result of this action by the pastor, her friend became severely ill and had to be hospitalized. KCL believed that her friend's sickness and hospitalization were due to the displeasure of the ancestors and gods:

> Yes . . . the pastor came . . . took the ancestral altars . . . the altars to the gods . . . all of them were burnt. How can this be good? As a result, her friend, not long after was admitted to the hospital . . . because he discarded all her gods and ancestral altars . . . you say, can this be good?

KC, while expressing her disapproval of such acts, also provided her perceptions on why the pastors throw or burn the images of the gods and altars—viewing these representations of spiritual realities as demonic:

> Christian pastors will only come in and throw away and dump your things. To them . . . all these are devils and satans. There are people who have warned me that the Christian pastors will just come in and throw your things.

Interestingly, KC also provided a helpful alternative for Christian pastors on how to properly remove the images and altars and what Taoists who have become Christians can offer to their ancestors (e.g., flowers) instead of usual food or burning of paper-made "daily necessities" (e.g., cars, cell phones, cash):

> We will have to send it off. And to send it off is a proper sending off . . . it is a formal occasion . . . a formal procession . . . that we are not just going to dump. We can't. Because we Chinese we believe in spirits and souls. Of course we got to send a Taoist priest . . . and to send off to the temple. And you still will visit the temples. But of course with flowers . . . by then let's say if I am a Christian . . . with flowers . . . and not with all those offerings anymore.

Emerging Domain: Appreciation

Inconsistency

Besides the various forms of condescension, many of the participants also expressed their disagreement with the ways Christians presented their spiritual realities. The participants pointed out that based on what they heard, these realities were inconsistent with what they perceive to be logical and helpful. For example, the participants highlighted the overemphasis on the removal of the consequences of an individual's sins or wrongdoing simply by asking for Jesus' forgiveness without talking about personal responsibility. Furthermore, they highlighted that Christian spiritual realities do not provide any practical insights for daily life. Thus, Christianity is not what the participants will turn to despite having visited churches for a number of times.

For PC, she pointed out that confession alone for sins committed is insufficient to remove the consequences:

> I hope you don't feel offended . . . is like what I said earlier—maybe they say that "Believe in me [i.e. Jesus] you will go to heaven . . . if you confess your sins that kind of thing. And then you will get rid or remove all sins and then you go to heaven that kind of thing" . . . but . . . I believe more in cause and effect in Buddhism or cause and fruit or retribution . . . so it is really cyclical in nature . . . which is true. Which is like sometimes it is also like common sense . . . which I feel that is very true. And I also believe that cause and effect or retribution is like you do that kind of sin, you will not simply say "I'm sorry . . . I confess . . . that kind . . . I will . . . straight away my sins will dissolve straight away." I will still suffer some kind of consequences unless I do some good deeds or whatever to minimize it or lessen that kind of effect.

In JK's experience, one of the reasons why she did not turn to Christianity during her personal crisis is because of the lack of emphasis by Christians on personal cultivation:

> Why didn't I look for Christianity? It is because Christianity is very childish. Christianity is all about the exterior. Every thing we just go and tell Jesus, beg him for help. I don't think that is the way. I think it should be that if I have any thing wrong within me . . . if there is something wrong with my thoughts . . . I need to look for a philosophy, a religion to solve the basic problems in how I think.

Finally for JE, Christian teachings and practices are not helpful in negotiating the anxieties of this present life:

The Dimensions That Establish And Sustain Religious Identity

> Okay . . . when we go to Taoist temple or Buddhist temple, in Taoism . . . we *bai bai*, draw divination sticks . . . you ask about things, you will go and draw divination sticks. Okay . . . he [priest or divining youth] will understand your issues. Regardless whether it is right or wrong, accurate or inaccurate, you will surely have an answer. When you go to the Buddhist temple, you will chant the *suttas*, end the cycle of life and death, hope that next time you will not be human . . . you want to be other things . . . you want to end the cycle of life and death. But when you go to the Christian [church] . . . they talk, talk, talk, sing, sing, sing and then suddenly stand up and shake hand . . . shake hand . . . like they are insane . . . this is the feeling they give me. When you go to the Buddhist temple, the things that they say, they are very practical . . . when there is cause, there is effect . . . something like that lor. What seed you plant . . . you will get what kind of fruit . . . this is the meaning. That is to say . . . what you do in your actions. But Christians . . . they don't have leh. They are only about forgiveness . . . continuously forgive, it doesn't matter what you do . . . you will be forgiven . . . ..

Discussion

This chapter has delineated how appreciation toward the power and presence of spiritual realities contributes toward sustaining the religious identity of the Buddhist and Taoist participants. Within their lives, the participants experienced transformation and protection, and received direction bestowed by the presence and power of these realities. Besides engaging in the sacred texts which provided them with insights to understand current and future realities and ethical principles to guide their behavior, and sacred acts to seek divine help during their times of need, the participants also witnessed sacred beings extending the necessary and timely assistance. As a result, they acknowledged their gratefulness toward these realities.

Data analysis also revealed another important subdomain that strengthened their appreciation of the teachings of Buddhism and Taoism and thereby sustaining their religious identity as Buddhists or Taoists—i.e., their disagreement over what the Christians said and did—in particular the cavalier attitude adopted by the Christians toward the physical representations of and places of residence for the spiritual realities highly regarded by the participants (e.g., the tablets or altars, images), the pressures exerted

Emerging Domain: Appreciation

by Christians during proselytizing, and the inconsistencies they encountered as they listened to the preaching in churches. Their expressions of disagreement, alongside unhappy sentiments, have also been highlighted recently in the local press and research.[3] The resulting tensions continue to present challenges toward future interreligious interactions and harmony in Singapore.

In the next chapter, I will present the final domain of dedication. This domain is primarily future-oriented—i.e., how the presence and power of spiritual realities serve to anchor the dedication of the participants and as a result undergird the participants' continued commitment to the respective religions. Two subdomains will be explored: aspiration and obligation. The aspiration subdomain revolves around the participants' desire to attain higher spiritual goals with the help of the different constituents of spiritual realities for their own well-being, as well as to be able to benefit others with their spiritual well-being. The obligation subdomain will reveal the participants' striving to extend the well-being dispensed by the power of these realities for those around them, such as family members and friends.

---

3. Lim, *NUS Orders Christian Group to Stop All Activities on Campus*. See also Robbie B.H. Goh, "Christian Identities in Singapore"; Kuah-Pearce, *State, Society, and Religious Engineering*, 279-289. See, "Building Bridges between Christians and Muslims" provides strategies to strengthen religious harmony in Singapore.

CHAPTER 7

EMERGING DOMAIN: DEDICATION

CHAPTERS 5 AND 6 have demonstrated how the recognition and appreciation of the power and presence of spiritual realities work to establish and sustain the religious identity of the Buddhist and Taoist participants. Yet, it needs to be pointed out that these domains are primarily centered upon the participants' past experiences with the realities. Thus, while these domains are still ongoing (i.e., the participants continue to recognize and appreciate these realities), they provide an incomplete picture of how spiritual realities will continue to sustain the religious identity of the participants in the days ahead. Here is where the dedication domain fills out the picture, as this domain is essentially anchored by the presence and power of spiritual realities to bring about a continuation of spiritual well-being offered by these realities for themselves, family, and friends. The various forms of well-being highlighted in this chapter are the dimensions the participants view as critical in undergirding their future commitment to these religions.

The insights for this chapter primarily arose during the concluding stages of each interview session, during which I asked the participants "Why Buddhism or Taoism in the days ahead?" Thus, while many of the participants reiterated what was mentioned and discussed under the domains of recognition and appreciation, there were also numerous occasions when they provided fresh perspectives as they responded to the question. Their perspectives can be categorized into two subdomains—aspiration and obligation.

EMERGING DOMAIN: DEDICATION

Dedication to the Enfolding Presence and Power of Spiritual Realities

Aspiration

The data revealed that the aspirations expressed by the participants are primarily self-oriented—i.e., the participants seeking to realize higher spiritual goals in their lives arising from their understanding of how spiritual realities can help them transcend their present selves and lessen the uncertainties associated with the life hereafter. At the same time, it is important to point out that their aspirations did not preclude their sense of responsibility to benefit others. In fact, I found that none of the aspirations are solely self-serving. Instead, as the participants strive to realize these goals in their lives, they are also mindful that the outcomes should also benefit others—for example promoting peaceful coexistence and keeping calm despite being on the receiving end of anger. This section will describe two forms of aspiration—personal and others-oriented.

Personal-oriented

The enfolding power and presence of spiritual realities to bring about personal well-being, both for this life and future ones, serves as a key dimension that sustains the religious identity of many of the participants in the days ahead. The participants alluded to several types of personal well-being. The first type is personal cultivation. For SL, she views Buddhism as a form of discipline that empowers her to cultivate her life through continuously removing the negative habits:

> Discipline is like . . . it is like when we are talking, there is meaning conveyed by our body, actions and words . . . this attitude toward others, thoughts or the way we talk . . . you will hurt others and also hurt yourself. This is the meaning conveyed by body, actions and words. It is here [in Buddhism] that if you slowly, slowly kick the habits . . . this becomes a way of life and then it turns into a changing point . . . then your life will turn around and you will be different.

In CN's life, mindfulness and *karma* act as deterrents to keep her conscientious not to engage in harmful actions that are contrary to the Five Precepts that she has vowed to observe:

> Mindfulness... okay... mindfulness... that means constant remind myself not to do something bad.... Ya... since young... or the effect of karma... believe in that because... you have to think twice... you have to think a lot before you want to do something bad....

JN described how her understanding of cause and effect and the Three Poisons, or *klesas* (ignorance, attachment, and aversion or hatred), helps her understand herself and also put herself in other people's shoes and thus keep from being angered easily:

> Buddhism they stress in self-practice, not just merely acquiring knowledge... but to test it out and know for yourself whether it works for you or not, whether it makes you a happier or peaceful person. So for instance, if... maybe somebody was to scold me, if a normal person will become angry very easily. Okay... but because we know things about karma or cause and effect ok, that is we begin to think "Eh... why is this person scolding me?" Maybe indeed I am really in the wrong, could it whether be it in the past or right here right now I have done something wrong. Ya... so we know things like the Three Poisons that causing us the suffering—greed, hatred, and ignorance. So we know that all these things... we have it... so other people will also have it. So when you think about all these things, you tend to like... will not blow up easily lah.

In LX's experience as a Taoist, she strives to be an upright person based upon what has been revealed to her by the *Dao de jing* through the practice of *bai bai*:

> Yes... *Dao de jing* [teaches]... how do we *bai* to the gods... just a very simple one... how do we hold the joss sticks. Holding the joss sticks, why do we hold them in front of our chest is because like during when we *bai*, we say it like "Oh... may our family experience peace"... is came out from our heart. So, from the heart, it all the way it rises all the way up... to send our message to the gods. Then why we hold the joss sticks, how we insert into the urn... cannot be like too deep... not too deep means our lives should not be overbearing... must have a sense of restraint... ah... that kind of thing. So sometimes I just find that this kind of thing is quite meaningful... teach us how to be a better person... not overbearing but must show a sense of restraint. Then, why must [joss sticks] be straight and not slanted? That is because our actions must be upright... do not do things that are underhanded.

Emerging Domain: Dedication

Besides personal cultivation, participants also aspire toward realizing personal happiness by learning not to hold onto things. According to SL, being able to repent before Buddha reminds her constantly to let things go. As such, she is becoming happier each day:

> It is because it has allowed me to be happy both physically and spiritually. My physical and spirit are both quite happy. You feel that your whole . . . after repentance, the entire condition of your spirit and your thinking are transformed . . . repentance is . . . like you did something wrong and you repent before Buddha . . . so that daily we will remember what wrongs have we done . . . so that it is necessary to change . . . must change.
>
> It allows us to know what is nothingness . . . that is to say we will not fight over different things with different people . . . like the insignificant issues . . . like we are acting in an ignorant way . . . So you will not be very picky . . . you will let go of many things. You will see these things as of little importance . . . not being as obsessive. Last time, I was very particular about everything, even when there is a small space that is not cleaned well. I was very particular and very angry. Now I am not longer like that . . . really I can feel it. I am completely different . . . unlike last time . . . every small thing I will say "No!" In this, I have changed a great deal. It is very beneficial for me. It allows me to be happy.

Participant MA also shared a similar journey, pointing to his adherence to the Five Precepts—i.e., abstinence from harming living beings, stealing, sexual misconduct, lying, and intoxication—as a lay follower that has helped him to lessen his cravings and anger. As a result, he is a much happier person and aspires to continue to be so:

> Ya . . . you really know . . . so far from . . . the day I started until now is like . . . I am less anger . . . less angry, less greedy and . . . and . . . it is very . . . you are really . . . you actually in fact getting happier everyday. So I think this is very important. Or else if you go to a religion and . . . you don't find answers and everything, I think that is quite bad for me . . . I feel . . . ya. I mean in life . . . to me . . . I just feel that . . . you stay in this world just to be happy lah.

As for KY, who is a Taoist, teachings in Taoism constantly remind him of the importance of contentment, which brings about joy. As a pragmatic person, he finds this reminder and other teachings to be pertinent in guiding his life. Thus, he sees himself as a committed practitioner in the days ahead.

The third type of personal-oriented aspiration is personal emancipation. In CW's understanding, personal direction is marked by overcoming *samsara* with the correct practice of the true and peaceful teachings of Buddha:

> Well, the path of peace . . . Okay . . . because this world that we live in is known as *samsara*. So there is a lot of unhappiness and in Buddhism we talk about Three Marks of Existence . . . that is the Impermanence, Un-satisfactoriness as well as Non-Self. So by learning these, I believe it would equip me on the path of peace. Not only the peace within myself, but also with others.

As for JK, her life is directed toward being free from future rebirths as a human. During the interview, she expressed her aspiration extensively with conviction:

> . . . when you go into it deeper and as you go further along . . . you will find that there is something deeper. What you seek is the goal outside of this human life. When you understand and you are freed . . . when you are freed yourself finally, maybe in your next life you do not need to be a human anymore. Because in our understanding, why we are humans is because we have karma . . . we have sins, like what God says—we have sins. So you return in this life . . . whether to repay debt . . . whether you give or take . . . it is all *karma*. So this is unending. In the next life, this will repeated. What you take, in your next life you will need to repay. When you repay, the next life you need to give. So when you learn it well, when you have gone beyond or surpassed, you can at the highest level, you can meditate until you surpass. You know that there are monks who go so deep into meditation that the person is no longer there . . . only the body is there. This is our goal . . . in the next life you don't need to be human anymore . . . no need to be human anymore. What could be better than this? You don't need to repay debts. Yes . . . because this life is suffering. In Buddhism, there is an important saying . . . life is suffering. In your suffering, you think it is happiness—money, position, wife, children. You think these will bring you happiness . . . but this is only temporary happiness. So do you know all these is suffering? So Buddha's best saying is this . . . human life is suffering not happiness. When you understand this . . . you seek to be freed. And to be free is not to be a human anymore.

Personal-oriented aspirations, especially with the objective of realizing personal well-being, happiness, and emancipation anchored by the

Emerging Domain: Dedication

presence and power of spiritual realities, provide a deeper understanding into how the dedication domain sustains the religious identity of the participants who are Buddhists or Taoists in the days ahead. YT's reflection of his journey as a Buddhist over the last six years serves as an excellent example that captures succinctly how personal-oriented aspirations sustain the religious identity of the participants. While he was "sick" (i.e., in the throes of mid-life crisis) some years ago, his engagement with the presence and power of spiritual realities helped him overcome the crisis. Having witnessed "the results . . . working for me," he noted that he would continue to walk the Buddhist path, as it will lead to "ultimate happiness":

> Basically, I see the results. You know, like the T-shirts they are selling—*Ehipassiko*—come and see for yourself. So I see the result is working for me. Just like when you are sick and you take this medicine . . . and this medicine works for you. So, you continue to take this medicine, right? So I believe that by walking this path, it will bring me to the ultimate happiness.

It is also worthwhile to be reminded that as the participants strive toward personal-oriented aspirations, they are conscientious in ensuring that the outcomes of their aspirations benefit the people around them. Thus, they are constantly mindful to establish peace with others, remain calm despite being misunderstood, and be upright in their behavior and interaction with others.

Others-oriented

While the personal-oriented aspirations fundamentally point to spiritual goals the participants are striving toward as Buddhists or Taoists, the others-oriented aspirations describe explicitly what the participants try or hope to do in order to extend spiritual wellness brought about by spiritual realities for the benefit of others. For a number of the participants, being able to better fulfill their roles as a son/daughter, parent, or member of society as a result of continually practicing spiritual insights derived from the sacred texts serves as a form of others-oriented aspiration. In Buddhism, this is known as "employing 'skillful means'"[1] in order to help others.

Thus, instead of the role determining religious identity as propounded by identity theory, what the participants revealed points to the

---

1. Williams, *Mahayana Buddhism*, 27.

opposite—i.e., the proper practice of the teachings in the sacred texts lead to the ability to play the role well. CW's views are insightful on this point. He noted that:

> Actually it is not the role played. It is what I contribute from learning Buddhism. Cause everyone has a role ... it is whether they play it well or play it badly. Ya ... I believe that by practicing Buddhism properly, one will be able to play the role well. Because the Buddha had in some *suttas* illustrate how a son would treat a parent. And the wife and the children and friends and society at large.

Similarly, YT also says Buddhism helped him enhance his roles:

> I don't see any conflict being a role of a son or a father or a ... husband, right? In fact, in Buddha's teachings himself, he taught a lot about how to be a good husband, how to be a good children, how to be a good parents, right ... how to be a good son as well ... In fact, it [Buddhism] does enhance your role.

For PC, she believes that the practice of Buddhism will bring about harmony in the roles that she plays. She remembered what her teacher taught her about the Buddhist way, which is to put harmonious relationships above the strict observance of Buddhist practices:

> ... my current teacher also says that sometimes you don't be so ... I can't remember the word she used. What she meant is sometimes you don't want to upset your family and all this, you shouldn't insist on practicing Buddhist things to upset them. Example she quoted is that a wife she refused to kill because her husband brought back some live food or something ... and want her to prepare a meal for him. Because of that, it may break the harmony. Undermine the husband-wife relationship because she says she is a Buddhist and does not want to kill live animals. She says to preserve family harmony, she can do it for her husband.

In order to extend spiritual well-being to the others around them besides their family members and friends, three of the participants also explicitly expressed their aspirations to be a nun, bodhisattva, and a lifelong assistant to a divining youth. For CN, having undergone a short-term ordination where she became a novice nun for two months, she aspires toward becoming a nun in order to help others:

> Because like what I say ... I am more into Buddhism for the past one and a half years after I took the Refuge. In fact I went for

Emerging Domain: Dedication

> this short-term orientation [ordination] last two months where I learnt quite a lot. Now I am thinking of long term if there is a chance. Now there are two masters who want to send me out to Taiwan or Malaysia for further study . . . hopefully two years later, the path is more obvious and if . . . if there is really this destiny for me to . . . to be a nun you know . . . I wish it will be in this life lah.

Furthermore, she also actively participates in the chanting sessions whenever any of her friends die, both to help the deceased as well as contribute back to the temple that has guided her learning and practice. During the interview, CN also showed me the marks made by joss sticks on her hands that were acquired during the ritual of 燃身供佛 (*ran shen gong fo,* or igniting the body as offering to the Buddha). She stated that in participating in this ritual, she is foregoing her "unwillingness to yield . . . an unyielding heart" so that she can be available to serve Buddhism for the rest of her life.

Similarly for JN, she desires to help others through her aspiration to follow the path of the bodhisattva as she sees the immense suffering associated with the cyclical rebirths that humans are subjected to. It must be pointed out that the path is not an easy one, and primarily consists of numerous arduous rebirths as well as practices. JN described her future path thusly:

> And the good thing is because Buddha taught about the path or he has given us the teachings on how we can practice in order to gain the true happiness or the final liberation from all these rebirth things. I see that it is really very suffering to go through al the rebirth cycles. So I will of course hope to get out of this cycle . . . ya . . . let's say I am able to get . . . perfect myself and get myself out of this cycle thing, I don't mind to say . . . come back and help others to pull them through this path [as a bodhisattva] also . . . But I have to be very strong first lah.

As for SYK, his desire is to serve humanity for the rest of his life through being an assistant to a divining youth. According to him, a divining youth's lifelong role is to serve others because the gods have chosen the divining youth to be their messengers in order to repay a debt owed in his previous life. Thus, SYK also sees his role as a lifelong calling:

> I am the first. From last time till now . . . my grandparents too . . . they did not have any association with *tiao tong* [divining youth] . . . completely no association. It is only me who has been

chosen. Usually this kind of *tiao tong* is they have inherited from the previous generation . . . passed on. For me, this is not the case. I am not related through blood . . . completely no prior relationship with them. I have already taken a vow . . . I have already said . . . until my last breath, I will serve Taoism . . . I will do until I can do no more . . . I do not do the *tiao tang* . . . I am just the assistant to the head . . . that is to say that when there is *tiao tong* . . . we are by their side [divining youth] . . . serving them and helping them. When he says how a charm is to be done, I need to write that out. That is to say that I am like a secretary . . . I write and tell the devotees how to use the charm.

The aspirations of the participants, the spiritual goals and well-being they seek for themselves and others, provide further insights into how the dedication domain works in tandem with the other domains of recognition and appreciation to sustain the religious identity of the participants. While the recognition and appreciation domains encompass the participants' past encounters with the presence and power of spiritual realities, the dedication domain is anchored by their desire to bring about spiritual wellness that is bestowed by these realities for themselves and others.

Obligation

Yet, at the same time, the aspirations expressed by the participants constitute only part of the overall insights provided by the participants in terms of why they will continue as adherents of Buddhism or Taoism. Another critical theme within the dedication domain is obligation. This subtheme primarily entails what the participants expressed as their responsibility to allay the anxieties arising from the life hereafter through dedicating themselves to continuously seek the well-being dispensed by the spiritual realities for their parents and ancestors.

The obligation highlighted by the participants is particularly pertinent for two reasons. First, within Singapore, the relationship between a parent and a child "is intimately linked to the notion of filial piety."[2] Filial obligation encompasses the children's moral responsibility to provide support to their elderly parents when they are alive out of honor and respect.[3] This support, particularly for the participants in this study, also includes

---

2. Goransson, *Binding Tie: Chinese Integrational Relations in Modern Singapore*, 10.
3. Ibid., 10.

Emerging Domain: Dedication

the spiritual. Thus, the participant guides their parents to take the Triple Refuge, and also engage in the ongoing accumulation and transference of merits for well-being of the parents.

Spiritual support, within the understanding of filial piety, does not end in this life. This leads to the second reason why obligation plays a key role in sustaining the religious identity of the participants. Arising from their recognition of the power of spiritual realities to bring about a better afterlife, the participants are duty-bound to look out for the welfare of their parents and ancestors after they have passed on through various ways. For the participants in this study, many of them pointed to the practices of offering food and other necessities made out of paper (e.g., clothing, shoes, money) and accumulating and transferring merits in order to shorten the suffering experienced in cyclical rebirths.

Obligation, in this study, points to the responsibility entrusted to the participants to extend various spiritual benefits—facilitated by the presence and power of spiritual realities in order to alleviate the uncertainties and fears arising from negotiating this life and what happens after death—to their parents and ancestors. Two categories emerged from the interviews: Present Life and After Life. Present life obligation is what the participants seek for the loved ones while the latter are still alive. The afterlife obligation points to what the participants seek on behalf of their deceased family members. For the rest of this section, I will explore the characteristics of these categories.

Present Life

For many of the participants, the notion of 回报 (*hui bao*, or the practice of return) undergird their attempts to seek assurances on behalf of their parents. *Hui bao*, a value emphasized by the Chinese, is intimately associated with filial piety. According to JK, this understanding is derived from the life cycle of a bird—the mother bird feeds the baby bird and when the latter grows up, the grown bird returns the favor by feeding the mother. Thus, JK brought her mother to take the Triple Refuge in accordance with her mother's destiny under the guidance of her master as part of her practice of return:

> Of course . . . I practice return . . . what I need to be done . . . I will do . . . I brought my mum to take the Refuge. My father has passed away . . . I am just following her destiny. I asked her "The master

> under whom I took the Refuge is very good. He has a Refuge ceremony... do you want to go?" Then my mum said "Okay... if you want to bring me there."... she feels that Buddhist is more suitable for her because she prays to *Guan yin*... Filial piety is extremely important. One should not stop being filial because of religion. I think this should be the way... more so since I am a Buddhist. In Buddhism, there is the emphasis on return.

According to AS, he pointed out that the act of leading one's parents to the Dharma and Triple Refuge while they are alive is the highest form of filial piety or return:

> In Buddhism, if you introduce something so good—the Dharma—to them and lead them into Buddhism, give them something for emotional support or help them to take the Refuge—this is immensely filial. A lesser form of filial piety is, in Buddhism, it is take care of his or her physical needs—clothes, food, accommodation, and transport, and then slowly moving to the immense filial piety. The in-between filial—I am not too sure. Immensely filial is to help them take the Refuge... nearly... I nearly fulfilled this wish of mine.

Although AS could not fulfill his wish as his father is hospitalized, he continues to encourage him to chant *Amitabha*. According to AS, this chant will help to bring about "infinite light" or understanding for the one who chants as he or she invokes the help of *Amitabha* Buddha.

Besides leading their parents to take the Refuge, another form of present-life obligation carried out by the participants for their parents, loved ones, or friends is the accumulation and transference of 功德 (*gong de*, or merits) to alleviate the ill-effects of bad *karma*. For PC, she witnessed how her accumulation and transference of merits to a hostile colleague resulted in a renewed and cordial working relationship:

> Transfer of merit is like let's say you do a good deed or whatever... you will say that "I wish the good merit gained can be transferred to those who are suffering or in hardship, hoping that the person will be happy and well." You transfer your merit or good deeds or merits that you have accumulated to the person that you feel that they need the credits and merits to let the person get better or happier. It is like you are sharing your merits with that person. Ya... it is like hope that she [the hostile colleague] is well and that she is not so troubled or mood swing that much that kind of thing.

Emerging Domain: Dedication

PC also delineated how the transference of merit works:

> It is just to chant in yourself . . . just think and say . . . thinking . . . not necessarily you have have to chant out loud . . . it is like you can think or meditate about it silently. When you do something good, you say "I wish to transfer my merits to this person . . . who is she and hope that she is well and happy that kind of thing."

PC's experiences with merit transfers are similar to what Xue Yu describes in his study into merit transfer within Theravada and Mahayana Buddhism. According to Yu, Buddhism developed the practice of merit transfer to overcome the uncertainty about what may happen after death. Furthermore, this notion has been particularly useful for the Chinese Buddhists as it provide "a special arena . . . to fulfill their filial piety through merit transfer."[4] He also notes that while merit transfer for the dead has overshadowed "the dynamic aspects of Buddhism for the living human beings,"[5] merit transfer is not solely for the dead. Merit transfer can also be practiced in the here and now to "improve the welfare of living beings and to enhance the relationship between human beings."[6]

Other participants also provided details of what they usually do to accumulate the merits that are to be transferred to their parents. The practices include participating in chanting sessions using *suttas* such as the Great Repentance *sutta* and Pure Land Past Life Divine *sutta*, and copying *suttas* in order to remove the bad *karma* in order to benefit their parents. This is the regular practice of AS despite what his father did to him:

> Nowadays, my responsibility is to copy the *suttas*, chant *Amitabha*, my daily merit, I transfer them to my parents—I do it continuously . . . I also copied a *sutta*, one copy for each of them. I am now starting to copy my fourth *sutta*. As you copy, you remove the bad *karma*. And slowly, the relationship will become better.

For CN, besides copying the *suttas*, she went a step further by participating in 燃身供佛 *ran shen gong fo*, or igniting the body as offering to the Buddha:

> Because I am now copying this *sutta* of the Bodhisattva *Guan yin* . . . the joss sticks markings on the arm . . . all these . . . this is during Vesak Day . . . during the orientation [ordination] . . . a

---

4. Yu, "Merit Transfer and Life after Death," 48.
5. Ibid., 49.
6. Ibid.

lot of people might misunderstand "Eh . . . tattoo or whatsoever." Actually it is a . . . I don't know if you have heard before . . . it is 燃身供佛 [*ran shen gong fo,* or igniting the body as offering to the Buddha] . . . an offering to Buddha. Actually it is not painful at all . . . So the true meaning of this is to tell people that . . . to sacrifice my inflexibility or unwillingness to yield. And you know . . . that means I forgo my body to make offering to the Buddha . . . another saying is that lessen the ill effects of *karma* . . . the ill effects of *karma* or you can use this as an offering to your parents.

The third type of present life obligation that the participants undertake for the sake of their parents is to demonstrate a commitment to continue the practice of these religions in order to honor the spiritual heritage of the ancestors and parents. For the participants, continuity of this heritage is tied strongly to both filial piety as well as the notion of 饮水思源 (*yin shui si yuan,* or remembering the source of the water that one drinks from). Commitment to this continuity, as a way of honoring the spiritual legacy of Taoism in Chinese culture and their own families, is particularly salient among the Taoist participants.

During my interviews with SY and KH, they were particularly assertive on this issue:

SY . . . that is our culture . . . by our roots . . . I do feel that we have to follow what our ancestors have done. You know . . . it is just like a tree . . . a tree without roots, the tree cannot survive. And the human is like a tree. You forget your roots, your roots being your ancestors . . . where they come from, how they nourished the whole family tree . . . So without going back to ancestors, going back to your roots, you will not succeed as the individual.

KH Taoism itself . . . in history and culture . . . it is something has been around for more than 4,000 years. Then father and ancestors, all of them are Taoists. That is it has been passed down till the present . . . we Singaporeans, the Chinese, or people of another religious affiliations, to have one concept—that is to remember 饮水思源 [*yin shui si yuan,* or remembering the source of the water that one is drinking] . . . remember where you came from, your roots . . . the concept behind these four words. Why must we talk about these four words . . . to remember the source of the water that you drink? Because of our ancestors, that is why we are here. From long ago, there are gods and deities and there are also legends about them . . . and in this manner passed down till today. So there is this need for continuity, how do you say that . . . must maintain . . . do not cut off this root . . . that is the most important.

It is no different for CT, as she pointed to the importance of continuity by inheriting the "family gods" passed down by her parents—i.e., gods and deities that her parents put up in their home:

> I see it as part of you . . . I mean the . . . the deities . . . the gods right . . . ya . . . so it's been like . . . you know . . . even for my parents . . . they will say that it is passed down . . . I mean, from their parents if they worship . . . so I see it . . . okay, in future . . . there is a need for me to continue that . . . practice.

During the interviews, I also encountered the use of "family gods" by other participants such as LX, SYK, and LC. According to them, these gods are part of the family, albeit highly revered. Thus, the participants pointed out that to *bai bai* before the gods before leaving and after coming each day is just like greeting a member of the family. For SYK, even though his aspiration is to serve as an assistant to the divining youth for the rest of his life, he noted that the importance of continuity by inheriting the gods and deities from his grandmother so that the "root will not be cut off."

After Life

The after life obligation points to what the participants seek to do to take care of the well-being of deceased family members and ancestors. A prominent way of ensuring the well-being of the deceased, via the accumulation and transference of merits, has been discussed previously. As pointed out by PC and CK, the merits that they accumulate are continuously transferred to their deceased loved ones in order to lessen the time spent in cyclical rebirths. For PC, besides transferring her merits to those around her, she also revealed that she is dedicated to the accumulation of merits so that these can be transferred to her deceased mother and sister in order to lessen their suffering:

> And this transfer of merits may not only be transferred to live persons only . . . for the dead persons . . . to my loved ones like my mum and my third sis[ter] . . . I wish them well and I hope that they will not suffer anymore in somewhere that kind of thing . . . so it encourages me to practice more good deeds.

In CK's experience, as a Buddhist, she was able to chant for her mother while her mother was close to death:

> My mum . . . my mum was on her deathbed already. Ya. And of course we believe that when we do chanting, we can help the deceased person . . . the one who is going to die . . . to cross over to the next world . . . ya. Oh . . . that is what we believe in . . . because chanting is also a merit. So it is called transference of merit to the person . . . to help the person.

Besides the accumulation and transference of merits, participants KL, KC, SW, KCL, and YN highlighted the importance of continuing to feed their late ancestors out of gratitude as well as honoring the practice that their parents passed on to them. As pointed out in chapter 5, these participants also highlighted the changes in taste of the food as evidence that the ancestors do eat the food. As a result, they are motivated and dedicated to ensure that their ancestors do not become "hungry ghosts."

For KC, she made a promise to her in-laws that she will ensure that the family's ancestors will be fed because all her children converted to Christianity. As a filial daughter-in-law, she pointed out that she intends to fulfill this promise for the rest of her life:

> I promised my parents-in-law . . . who are in their 90s and 80s that I will continue to bring down . . . carry on the Lai ancestors . . . to do offerings to them. But until my generation right, that shall be the end because my children and the . . . family . . . besides the old couple, all of them are . . . Christians. So ultimately, this is the main concern of my mother-in-law because she feels that she will be left out . . . there will be nobody that will offer to pray . . . to continue . . . ya . . . it is a promise to them. And I behave as a filial . . . as a filial daughter-in-law.

As for SW, KCL, and YN, they pointed out ensuring that their ancestors are fed is both an obligation as well as an expression of gratitude:

> Our thinking is like this . . . one generation passes on to the next generation . . . that is to say last time, they also *bai* [in the form of offering food] their ancestors in this manner. Now that my parents have passed on, for us it [offering food] is a token . . . an expression of our gratitude in our hearts.

It is also noteworthy to point out that despite the dedication by these participants to ensure that their ancestors are fed in the afterlife—either out of promise, gratitude, or responsibility—none of the participants expect their children to do the same for them. In fact, when I asked MQ, KC, SW, KCL, and YN if they are worried that they will be "hungry ghosts," they all pointed out that they have "no choice" as they cannot force their children to feed them after their deaths. Thus, they leave everything in the hands of destiny for their well-being in the life hereafter.

Discussion

The dedication domain serves to complete the picture of how the enfolding presence and power of spiritual realities serve to sustain and establish the religious identity of the Chinese Singaporeans who are Buddhists or Taoists. With dedication firmly rooted in these realities that will be able to bring about an ongoing well-being for themselves and their family members (deceased or otherwise), the religious identity of the participants is sustained. Thus, the participants aspire toward personal cultivation, happiness, and emancipation. At the same time, they also dedicate themselves to faithfully carry out their obligation to accumulate and transfer merits, offer food, and carry on the family religion for their family members' (deceased or otherwise) well-being and honor.

In the next chapter, I will conclude my theory of the *Enfolding Presence and Power of Spiritual Realities* as an overarching idea that best explains the dimensions that establish and sustain the religious identity of Chinese Singaporeans who are Buddhists or Taoists. The chapter will begin with a brief summary of the underpinning domains of the theory as a way of illustrating how these domains work together to provide richer insights into the religious identity of the Buddhists and Taoists. Subsequently, it will highlight the implications arising from this study for two areas—research and practice. Finally, the chapter concludes with various possibilities for further study.

CHAPTER 8

THE CENTRALITY OF SPIRITUAL REALITIES IN RELIGIOUS IDENTITY

THE VITALITY OF BUDDHISM and Taoism and the practices and rituals associated with these traditional Chinese religions have not abated amongst Chinese Singaporeans despite Singapore's rapid modernization and transformation in its sociocultural, political, and economic landscapes. This study has demonstrated that a ground-up approach utilizing a broadened conceptualization of religious identity as an analytical construct generates robust and illuminating insights as to why Chinese Singaporeans continue to adhere to Buddhism or Taoism through a deeper understanding of the dimensions that undergird their commitment.

To discover and explain the dimensions that establish and sustain the religious identity of the participants, in essence, calls for sensitivity to two critical facets—(a) the pervasive presence and power of metaphysical or spiritual constituents inherent within these religions, and (b) the fundamental characteristics of identity. Furthermore, this process must also be rooted in the perspectives of the adherents instead of solely examining the impact of societal or external forces.

Throughout this study, religious identity is viewed as a distinct facet of identity that is intersected by the overlapping entities of religion and identity and consists of the respective salient characteristics of these entities. Thus, it is defined as an individual's awareness of and commitment to (a) a continuous and invigorating inner well-being, and (b) a sense of belonging and desire to extend the well-being to the sociocultural community associated with the divine. This awareness and commitment arises out of an individual's reciprocal interactions with the divine and the sociocultural community associated with the divine.

Sensitivity to these salient characteristics did not mean that this study intentionally set out to validate the contributions of the spiritual realities in establishing and sustaining the religious identity of the participants and in the process ignore the impact of societal factors. Instead, this study began with the purpose of discovering and explaining the dimensions that undergird the religious identity of the participants, guided by the above definition and the existing gaps within the current studies described in chapters 1, 2, and 3.

Thus, not surprisingly, the participants did point to the impact of the societal or external dimensions upon religious identity during the interviews. These dimensions included (a) relationships—the influence of parents and friends; (b) structures and services—temples and organizations (e.g., Buddhist Fellowship, Buddhist Library) in providing courses, seminars, free materials, and a place for meditation, chanting, and *bai bai*, and the performance of key rituals; (c) ethnicity—being a Chinese necessitates or strengthens one's commitment to either being a Buddhist or Taoist; and (d) familial and cultural values—expectations associated with the Chinese community, such as filial piety and respect.

These societal dimensions cannot be dismissed as insignificant, as they cohere with the consensus of existing research. However, what emerged prominently from the analysis of the data is the numerous ways in which spiritual realities intersected with the lives of the participants. As a result, societal dimensions came to play a twofold supporting role. The first role is that of a scaffold, providing a framework that afforded the participants opportunities to encounter the power and presence of spiritual realities. As a result of their encounters, the participants experienced inner well-being and rejuvenation. The second role is that as a base for the participants to extend the well-being brought about by the realities for the sake of their parents and ancestors in the life hereafter. The culmination of experiencing and extending spiritual well-being results in the strengthening of their commitment to remain as adherents of the religions in the days ahead.

The Enfolding Presence and Power of Spiritual Realities in Establishing and Sustaining Religious Identity

The central theory that emerged from the data that best explains the dimensions that establish and sustain the religious identity of Chinese Singaporeans who are either Buddhists or Taoists is the *Enfolding Presence and Power of Spiritual Realities*. The spiritual realities that exert prominent influence in the lives of the participants include (a) sacred acts such as *bai bai*, chanting, and meditation; (b) sacred beings or forces who interacted with the participants and also whom the participants interacted with; and (c) sacred texts such as *suttas* and the *Dao de jing* that guided the participants with transcendent insights to negotiate tensions and anxieties associated with present and future realities.

This theory proposes that religious identity is established and sustained by the realities' enfolding presence and power as the participants immersed themselves in the domains of recognition, appreciation, and dedication. The theory can be depicted as dynamic in nature primarily due to the reciprocal interactions that took place within these domains. Through their participation in sacred acts such as *bai bai* and rituals before sacred beings such as Buddha or Taoist gods and deities in temples, the participants came to recognize the presence and power of these realities especially during times of need or crises. At the same time, the recognition of these realities also took place when the realities, in particular sacred beings or forces, revealed themselves to the participants.

Upon turning to these realities for help, the participants experienced much-needed and timely assistance. The forms of assistance included transformation, direction, and protection, which further demonstrated the availability and ability of these realities to bring about enduring well-being and safety for the participants. The assistance extended by these realities generated a deep sense of appreciation in the participants. The domain of appreciation is also further strengthened by the participants' disagreement with the ways Christians responded toward the physical representations of sacred realities that are highly esteemed by the Taoists or Buddhists, and the Christians' expression of the teachings recorded in the Bible.

Besides the recognition of and appreciation toward the presence and power of spiritual realities serving to establish and sustain the religious identity of the participants, the dedication domain revealed how these realities will sustain their religious identity into the future. This domain is largely characterized by aspiration and obligation, although a number of the participants also reiterated their recognition of and appreciation toward these realities as strong foundations to ensure that they remain as Buddhists or Taoists for the rest of their lives. It is noteworthy to point out that the participants' aspirations are not exclusively self-serving. The participants were also mindful that the outcomes of their aspirations must benefit those around them and they also sought to extend the well-being imparted by spiritual realities for their deceased parents and ancestors as part of demonstrating filial piety.

Recognition

The recognition domain is characterized by the participants becoming acquainted with the power and presence of spiritual realities as they participated alongside parents or friends in the various rituals and practices at temples or homes. Most of the participants recalled the numerous occasions their parents brought them along to *bai bai*, or chanting sessions, at different temples in order to seek blessings or help, and also included them in the preparations for the rituals during key occasions.

For a number of them, although the participation with their parents was highlighted as unhelpful experiences in that what their parents did was ritualistic, these experiences nevertheless motivated them to search for the truer form of Buddhism or Taoism that focuses more on understanding the teachings from the sacred texts. With the help of friends, they came into contact with this form of Buddhism or Taoism. Research by John Clammer and Khun Eng Kuah-Pearce has identified this form of Buddhism as Reform Buddhism, one that is aligned closely with Theravada Buddhism. Within Taoism, it is known as philosophical Taoism due to the focus on the *Dao de jing*, as opposed to religious Taoism that focuses more on rituals and the use of *zhou* or mantra-like chants.[1]

With this acquaintance of the presence and power, the participants knew who to turn to or what to do in times of need or crises—for example which deity to go to for a specific need and turning to meditation during the lowest points in their lives. As the participants sought the help of the spiritual realities, the latter extended assistance to the former. Thus, not only did the participants gain further affirmation of the presence and power of spiritual realities, they were also deeply appreciative of the divine help given.

1. Lee et al., *Taoism*, 126–31.

The recognition of the presence and power of spiritual realities also took place via revelation. The revelation theme points to spiritual realities disclosing themselves to the participants in a variety of forms. The most prominent one highlighted by the majority of the participants is destiny, which the participants point out is the result of the accumulation of good merits or *karma*, past practice of Buddhism in previous lives, and being responsive to spontaneous occurrences in life. Thus, with destiny being closely intertwined with the participants' practices in their previous lives, coming into contact with and feeling a deep sense of belonging to these religions in this life is a blessing. Since destiny has blessed them, the participants believe that it is critical to continue to follow destiny's path for the rest of their lives.

Besides destiny, the participants also witnessed the different ways in which spiritual realities made themselves known. These ways of manifestation, which a number of participants viewed as a form of destiny, include the appearances of sacred beings in dreams, the emitting of a mysterious force, stimulus-response, and miraculous acts. These encounters were so vivid that, together with destiny, they became significant themes that established and sustained their religious identity.

Appreciation

Within this domain, the participants acknowledged their appreciation for the concrete help and responses given by the spiritual realities. The help and responses experienced by the participants encompass transformation, direction, and protection. Inner renewals that enabled the participants to overcome personal crises and negative attitudes characterize the transformation subdomain. The direction subdomain is marked by the participants gaining insights from the sacred texts that enable them to understand the realities beyond what they could see, as well as ethical guidelines for them to live in light of these realities. Besides inner renewal, the participants also pointed out their appreciation for the protection offered by spiritual realities—which included daily safety as well as the specific intervention in delivering their loved ones from physical harm.

While the participants' appreciation toward the realities enfolded within Buddhism and Taoism mainly came about because of the help rendered, their appreciation is also further strengthened by their disagreement with the ways Christians in Singapore responded toward these realities.

The Centrality of Spiritual Realities in Religious Identity

From criticizing the *jing shen* or literally the "pure body" (term used by Taoists to describe the statue or image) of the gods as simply made out of wood, to dumping or burning these alongside ancestral tablets and pressuring the participants to convert, all these actions were viewed unfavorably by the participants and inevitably stirred up sentiments of unhappiness and resentment. In fact, a number of participants pointed out that they have often chased Christians away when the Christians attempted to convert them. Finally, a number of the participants also pointed out that teachings from the Bible do not align with what they perceive to be reality. As such, the spiritual realities presented by the Christians did not make sense to the participants and are not helpful from their perspective in negotiating the anxieties associated with the present life.

Dedication

Besides the recognition and appreciation of how the presence and power of spiritual realities have contributed to the participants' well-being, coupled with their disagreement with, and negative sentiments toward, what the Christians did and said, dedication to these realities is another critical aspect revealed by them. Within this domain, the participants devote themselves to extend the continuous well-being provided by spiritual realities for themselves and those around them. Their dedication is rooted in their understanding of the ever-ready help that is found in these realities. Thus, the domain is distinguished by the participants' aspiration and obligation.

Aspiration consists of a twofold orientation—personal and others. The former points to the participants aspiring to realize higher spiritual goals in their lives so that they can continue to experience the inner stability and wellness (e.g., happiness, removal of negative habits) from their past encounters with spiritual realities. At the same time, as they seek to attain higher spiritual goals, the participants are also fully aware of the need to benefit others. Thus, they pointed out how the realization of these spiritual realities in their own lives (e.g., living out the teachings of the sacred texts, becoming a nun or bodhisattva) can benefit those around them—such as becoming better at fulfilling their various roles and responsibilities, and being able to help others negotiate the tensions in this life and the life hereafter.

Obligation, which is rooted in the value of filial piety, points to the responsibility entrusted to the participants to provide for the spiritual well-being of their parents or immediate family, both in this life and the next. Besides filial piety, the participants are also guided by their recognition of the power of spiritual realities to bring about a better afterlife if they faithfully carry out the related practices or rituals (e.g., accumulating and transferring of merits, offering of food during key occasions). The obligation theme also consists of a twofold orientation—present life and after life.

In carrying out the present life obligation, the participants sought to do one or more of the following: bringing their parents to take the Triple Refuge (as this act is considered an exemplary form of filial piety), accumulating and transferring merits to their parents to lessen their bad *karma*, and committing to carry on the spiritual heritage of their parents. As for the afterlife obligation, the participants dedicate themselves to an ongoing accumulation and transference of merits, as well as sustenance of their deceased family members (e.g., through offering of food).

The aspiration and obligation subdomains reveal that in the participants' perception, spiritual well-being exists in a continuum between this life and the next through the ongoing mediation by spiritual realities. There is a need for the participants to ensure that this well-being is experienced in this life and the next by their loved ones and themselves. Thus, it is of no surprise that the participants dedicate themselves to be Buddhists or Taoists for the rest of their lives.

Implications of Study

This study has delineated the dimensions that establish and sustain the religious identity of Chinese Singaporeans who are either Buddhists or Taoists. By listening to experiences of the participants, it has provided a fresh perspective to the ever-expanding body of research into religious identity emerging both from Singapore and the wider body of theories of identity. There are a number of implications arising from this study for future research as well as practice.

Implications for Research

Participants

Through this study, the participants' views and experiences with spiritual realities have been affirmed as critical contributions to the current academic research on religious identity and religions emerging from Singapore. While the current studies have overwhelmingly discussed the direct correlation between the impact of external factors (e.g., societal transformations, government intervention, and structural renewals undertaken by the respective religions) and the strength of the religious identity of the Buddhist and Taoist communities, listening to the internal narratives of the participants reveals the significance of their daily interactions with the presence and power of spiritual realities embedded within these religions.

Furthermore, their stories and voices have generated richer insights toward filling the gaps that exist within the current research in the following ways. First, the experiences of the participants validated this study's proposal for the definition and conceptualization of religious identity to encapsulate the salient characteristics within the two overlapping entities that make up the construct—religion and identity. Thus, religious identity should neither be used conjointly as a social or group identity, nor loosely as equivalent to religiosity or religious identification.

Second, the participants' narratives have also provided useful resources to bring about greater understanding in terms of the dimensions that establish and sustain the participants' inner wholeness and rejuvenation and commitment to these religions. A deeper understanding of these highly regarded and significant dimensions and their roles can sensitize other religious adherents to respond appropriately toward these dimensions. Third, as discussed previously, the participants' voices have provided impetus for research to look beyond the external or visible factors in understanding how religious identity is established and sustained for Chinese Singaporeans who are either Buddhists or Taoists.

Research in Singapore

This study has revealed that the dimensions that establish and sustain religious identity are complex and multilayered. Besides the presence of various societal dimensions as pointed out earlier in this chapter, the participants also encountered, experienced, and continue to commit to the enfolding presence and power of spiritual realities, such as the guidance of destiny, gods, and deities within the Taoist pantheon, accumulation and transference of merits, and realization of teachings from the sacred texts into daily living for continuous well-being.

Thus, an understanding of the presence and power of these realities has provided the impetus for future research in Singapore related to the religious identity of Singaporeans to be cognizant of these dimensions. During the interviews, when the participants were asked "Why Buddhism or Taoism for yourself?," "In what ways have Buddhism or Taoism been meaningful for yourself?," and "Why Buddhism or Taoism for yourself in the days ahead?," their responses overwhelmingly pointed to the power and presence of spiritual realities in their lives. Ah Eng Lai astutely notes that in Singapore, despite the major role played by the government in the lives of Singaporeans, religions and religious communities continue to "have their own worlds and realities which offer motivations, fulfillments, [and] meanings"[2] for the adherents. Thus, it is critical that local research be sensitive to these realities in order to better capture the breadth and depth of religious experiences existing on the island.

At the same time, this study has also demonstrated the value of approaching the issue of religious identity using a qualitative approach. Qualitative study enables a researcher to capture the realities on the ground, in this case rich internal narratives that reflect the participants' experiences as Buddhists and Taoists negotiating Singapore's multireligious landscape. These experiences, as delineated by this study, include well-being and rejuvenation as well as negative stereotyping. Insights generated by these narratives can enrich the existing pool of knowledge about religious experiences and diversity in Singapore, which in turn can be drawn upon by other religious organizations or communities that seek to work toward strengthening future interreligious interactions and understanding for the well-being of everyone living in Singapore.

Research in Theories of Identity and Religious Identity

This study, conducted among Chinese Singaporeans who are Buddhists or Taoists, has also broadened the current Western-dominated conceptualizations of identity and religious identity by providing non-Western perspectives and insights. As discussed in chapters 1 and 3, existing research on theories of identity dominated by Western constructs has largely overlooked the inclusion of interactions with the divine or sacred because these interactions do not fit within a rational understanding of identity formation.[3]

---

2. Lai, "Conclusion," 692.
3. King, "Religion and Identity," 198; Hopkins, "Religion and Social Capital," 538;

The Centrality of Spiritual Realities in Religious Identity

Identities—religious or otherwise—do not exist apart from social practices and societal forces.[4] However, from the narratives of the participants in this study, social practices or structures are not the sole dimensions that establish and sustain religious identity. The presence and power of spiritual realities such as sacred beings, texts, and acts also play significant roles.

Furthermore, religious identity does not only revolve around individuals' self-fulfillment. Instead, participants perceive the dedicating of oneself to extend spiritual benefits bestowed by spiritual realities for others—both the living and the dead—as a significant process. Finally, the role of the divine or spiritual should not be set aside in favor of rational explanations. This study has highlighted that for Chinese Singaporeans who are Buddhists or Taoists, daily or regular experiences with spiritual realities are an integral and necessary part of being adherents of these religions.

Implications for Practice

Besides implications for research, this study also provides various considerations for practice, in particular for Christians in Singapore. The need to devote attention to practice in this section arises for two key reasons.

First, Singapore's dynamic and diverse religious landscape has not experienced any violent religious conflicts since independence in 1965. Yet, such a landscape does not preclude the presence of underlying religious competition and occasional distrust and misunderstanding between religious groups, often brought about by ignorance, stereotyping, and insensitive interreligious encounters. It does not mean such peace can be taken for granted. Singapore is not immune from the "rise of religious fundamentalism [and] powerful transnational associational pulls with renewed religiosity of the various mainstream faiths."[5] Religious identity, much like other forms of identity (e.g., ethnic, national, cultural), has the potential to bring about inclusion and well-being as well as exclusion and hostility.[6] Thus, there is a need to ensure that religious identity "sit comfortably with the larger interests of social cohesion, national unity and the common good of society."[7]

Merriam, *Non-Western Perspectives on Learning*, 5.
    4. Bidwell, "Practicing the Religious Self," 3-4.
    5. Tan, "Keeping God in Place," 58.
    6. Ashmore et al., "Introduction," 3. See also Volf, *Exclusion and Embrace*, 20.
    7. Lai, "Conclusion," 691.

Second, while the Singapore government has put in place strict institutional and legal policies to safeguard interreligious harmony and a number of national committees (e.g., Inter-Religious Organization or IRO and Inter-Racial Confidence Circles or IRCCs) and to promote interreligious dialogues, "much is left to religious organizations, groups, and individuals themselves to initiate and participate in interfaith dialogues and collaboration."[8] The sustainability and success of such efforts rest largely on how these organizations, groups, and individuals can set the example of how to "make peace and achieve harmonious living."[9]

In light of these reasons, attention must be given to the cultivation of practice. Practice is defined here as ways of talking and being arising from learning and interaction within a specific cultural context that enable individuals to foster peaceful and harmonious relationships within their social spaces.[10] It is an embodied set of ethical actions that are reflective of the character of individuals.

With practice arising from learning and through interaction, what kind of learning will enable an individual to imbibe and enact such ethical actions? Furthermore, what kind of attitudes need to undergird ongoing interaction such that an individual's talking and being promotes peaceful and harmonious relationships?

Duane Elmer puts forth a compelling learning model, which comprises three types of learning—*about others, from others,* and *with others.* He states that these types of leaning are a form of ability, primarily because it is "something that we can do, do better, and even master."[11] At the most basic level is learning about others. This type of learning helps to form understanding and appreciation, and it primarily takes place at a distance because it entails the process of finding out through interacting with a medium (e.g. lectures, books, films, internet).

Through interviewing the Buddhist and Taoist participants, this study points to the power and presence of spiritual realities as the key dimensions that establish and sustain the religious identity of the participants. It also sheds light into the participants' experiences with these dimensions in the context of their everyday lives, for example the daily *bai bai* with

---

8. Ibid., 692.

9. Ibid., 693.

10. See Dykstra and Bass, "Foreword," viii; Jarvis, *Human Learning,* 13; Volf, *Exclusion and Embrace,* 29.

11. Elmer, *Cross-Cultural Servanthood,* 93.

The Centrality of Spiritual Realities in Religious Identity

the use of joss sticks, the importance of Five Precepts and Eightfold Path, and numerous encounters with destiny, gods, and deities. As such, these findings provide a good start for the other religious communities to learn more about the diverse dimensions that undergird the religious identity of Buddhists and Taoists.

Yet, this type of learning—i.e., about others, has limited effectiveness in transforming practice, primarily because such learning is confined to the taking in of information.[12] There is a need for Christians to pursue the other learning processes of learning from and with Buddhists and Taoists about the significance of spiritual realities. According to Elmer, learning from others entails asking questions, seeking understanding, and probing the thoughts of others. Elmer goes on to point out that these acts of listening demonstrate "respect for the speaker and helps to build a sense of community."[13] As for learning with, it occurs "in relationship, in mutuality, in partnership where neither side is above or beneath."[14]

Learning from and with each other will inevitably foster a deeper understanding of, and improve responses toward, Buddhists and Taoists. Such interdependence and interconnectedness in learning calls for humility in order to explore how spiritual realities bring about well-being in Buddhists' and Taoists' lives (e.g., work, family, relationships). Furthermore, it also calls for an inquisitive attitude to ensure that such learning is ongoing and becomes an integral part of these communities' practices. For the Buddhists and Taoists, reciprocal humility and inquisitiveness will help to generate a deepened understanding of the dimensions that shape the religious identity of other religious adherents and cultivate the practice of Buddhists and Taoists as well.

Where can adherents of other religions engage in these two learning processes? Etienne Wenger suggests it is within the preexisting relationships that are forged through participating in various communities of practice (CoP). In these CoPs, individuals learn from each other as they engage in various daily enterprises—from "ensuring our physical survival to seeking the most lofty pleasures."[15] Thus, CoPs are everywhere and everyone belongs to several CoPs at any time.

---

12. Ibid., 93. Also Jarvis, *Human Learning*, 28. He categorizes such learning as non-reflective learning.

13. Ibid., 98.

14. Ibid., 103.

15. Wenger, *Communities of Practice*, 45

As the individual participates in CoPs, learning takes place as it is "not a separate activity... something we do when we do nothing else."[16] Learning is not an exclusively academic enterprise within an academic context. Rather, it occurs in the context of our experiences as we participate in the world. For example, a father chats with other fathers in the neighborhood about the best ways to raise children. At the same time, he is also an engineer in his workplace working with fellow engineers to develop the latest software, and a member of a local volunteer group helping the elderly. Thus, these CoPs often become natural spaces of convergence for adherents of various religions.

Within Singapore, it is not difficult to come into contact with Buddhists and Taoists in various CoPs—such as where we live, work, study, relax, or volunteer. The key question is how can Christians become intentional in learning about the presence and power of spiritual realities that serve to sustain the Buddhists' and Taoists' religious identity? In the course of daily interactions and conversations, is it possible for Christians to encourage Buddhists and Taoists to share about their experiences with the spiritual realities in order to foster genuine conversations? Might important days commemorated by Buddhists and Taoists (e.g., Vesak, Seventh Month Festival) be opportunities for other religious adherents to learn from Buddhists and Taoists? Similarly for adherents of Buddhism or Taoism, will reciprocal learning from and with the adherents of other religions lead to greater clarity about the spiritual realities central to other religions? Over the course of time, might not these engagements that are undertaken with humility and a desire to learn make a more harmonious society?

Recommendations for Further Study

While this study has provided a theory that explains the dimensions that establish and sustain the religious identity of Chinese Singaporeans who are either Buddhists or Taoists, it also reveals a number of areas that require further research. First, this study is confined to Chinese Buddhists and Taoists who are born and raised in Singapore. What about Chinese Buddhists and Taoists who were born and raised outside of Singapore but later migrated to the island? What are the dimensions that undergird their religious identity? Specifically, how did the power and presence of spiritual realities help them to negotiate their uncertainties and anxieties as immigrants?

16. Ibid., 8.

The Centrality of Spiritual Realities in Religious Identity

Second, what are the dimensions that establish and sustain the religious identity of the adherents of other religions (e.g., Christianity, Islam, Hinduism) in Singapore? Using this renewed conceptualization of religious identity as an analytical construct, what insights can we glean by interviewing these adherents? How will the adherents describe the role of the divine or spiritual realities? What will be the similarities and differences in terms of the dimensions?

Third, in light of the strength of the enfolding presence and power of spiritual realities to undergird religious identity, it will be instructive to find out why Chinese Buddhists and Taoists choose to leave these religions. What are the dimensions that bring about a shift in commitment? How do the spiritual realities in Buddhism or Taoism act as push factors and the realities in other religions serve as pull factors?

Finally, within the Buddhist and Taoist communities in Singapore, various schools or traditions exist. By interviewing Buddhists and Taoists according to their traditions, such as Mahayana, Theravada, Vajrayana, 全真 (*Quan zhen*, or Complete Perfection) and 正一 (*Zhen yi*, or Orthodox Unity), how will the insights generated from these comparative studies further enrich our understanding of the dimensions that establish and sustain religious identity? Will certain constituents of spiritual realities be more prominent for certain schools vis-à-vis other schools?

Conclusion

Being etic to the world of Buddhism and Taoism, embarking on this research as a learner has afforded me numerous opportunities to both learn about Buddhism and Taoism through a survey of existing literature, as well as learn from the participants through asking questions and seeking understanding and clarification. While the *learning about* process provided me with the much-needed background information, it was through the *learning from* process that I had the privilege to be able to listen in to the participants' fascinating and insightful narratives that detailed their encounters and experiences with the presence and power of spiritual realities. Their voices, in many ways, injected a dynamic element into what I have read, and more importantly, fresh perspectives on the understanding of the dimensions that establish and sustain religious identity.

At the same time, their patient elucidation has enlightened my ignorance of these intricate and complex realities. Admittedly, there remains

The Dimensions That Establish And Sustain Religious Identity

much to be understood in terms of the dimensions that establish and sustain the religious identity of Chinese Singaporeans who are Buddhists or Taoist, for me and many of the adherents of other religions in Singapore. This understanding can only be achieved if we continue to learn about, from, and with the Buddhist and Taoist communities, and vice versa. Such collaborative learning encounters will hopefully expand our understanding of each other and in turn necessitate a readjustment within each of our practices toward each other. Only then will we be able to continuously make space for each other's religious identities as we continue to live and share a multireligious environment within this small nation-state.

Appendix A

Sample Interview Guide

1. What draws you to Buddhism or Taoism?
2. When are the times or occasions in your life in which Buddhism or Taoism have been especially meaningful? How has Buddhism or Taoism been meaningful?
3. What makes you choose and continue to practice Buddhism or Taoism?
4. How important is your family/extended family/friends/colleagues in your choice or continued practice of Buddhism or Taoism?
5. How do the roles you play (e.g. son, daughter, parent, student) or obligations that you have (e.g. familial duties) affect your choice or continued practice of Buddhism or Taoism?
6. How does the Buddhist or Taoist community contribute toward your choice or continued practice of Buddhism or Taoism?
7. What comes to your mind when you say you are a practitioner of Buddhism or Taoism?
8. How do your actions/interactions demonstrate that you are a practitioner of Buddhism or Taoism?

Bibliography

Abrams, Dominic. "Social Identity, Social Cognition, and the Self: The Flexibility and Stability of Self-Categorization." In *Social Identity and Social Cognition*, edited by Dominic Abrams and Michael A. Hogg, 197–229. Malden, MA: Blackwell, 1999.

Abrams, Dominic, and Michael. A Hogg. "Collective Identity: Group Membership and Self-Conception." In *Self and Social Identity*, edited by Marilyn B. Brewer and Miles Hewstone, 147–81. Malden, MA: Blackwell, 2004.

Ashmore, Richard D., and Lee Jussim. "Introduction: Toward a Second Century of the Scientific Analysis of Self and Identity." In *Rutgers Series on Self and Social Identity: Vol. 1. Self and Identity: Fundamental Issues*, edited by Richard D. Ashmore & Lee Jussim, 3–19. New York: Oxford University Press, 1997.

Ashmore, Richard. D., et al. "Introduction: Social Identity and Intergroup Conflict." In *Rutgers Series On Self And Social Identity: Vol. 3. Social Identity, Intergroup Conflict and Conflict Resolution*, edited by Richard. D. Ashmore et al., 3–14. New York: Oxford University Press, 2001.

Auerbach, Carl F., and Louise B. Silverstein. *Qualitative Data: An Introduction to Coding and Analysis*. New York: New York University Press, 2003.

Balkin, Richard S., et al. "Religious Identity and Cultural Diversity: Exploring the Relationship between Religious Identity, Sexism, Homophobia, and Multi-cultural Competence." *JCD* 87 (2009) 420–27.

Beit-Hallahmi, Benjamin. "Religion and Identity: Concepts, Data, Questions." *SSI* 30 (1991) 81–95.

Bell, David. M. "Religious Identity: Conceptualization and Measurement of the Religious Self." PhD diss., Emory University, 2009.

Berger, Peter L. "Modern Identity: Crisis and Continuity." In *The Cultural Drama, Modern Identities, and Social Ferment*, edited by Wilton S. Dillon, 159–81. Washington, DC: Smithsonian Institution, 1974.

———. *The Sacred Canopy: Elements of a Sociological Theory of Religion*. New York: Anchor, 1969.

Berger, Peter L., and Thomas Luckmann. *The Social Construction of Reality: A Treatise in the Sociology of Knowledge*. New York: Anchor, 1966.

Berkel, LaVerne A., et al. "Similarities and Differences between Religiosity and Spirituality in African American College Students: A Preliminary Investigation." *Counseling and Values* 49 (2004) 2–14.

Bhaskar, Roy. *From Science to Emancipation: Alienation and the Actuality of Enlightenment*. New York: Routledge, 2012.

Bibliography

Bidwell, Duane. R. "Practicing the Religious Self: Buddhist-Christian Identity as Social Artifact." *Buddhist-Christian Studies* 28 (2008) 3–12.

Blumer, Harold. *Symbolic Interactionism.* Englewood Cliffs, NJ: Prentice-Hall, 1969.

Boys, Mary C. *Maps and Visions: Educating in Faith.* Lima, OH: Academic Renewal, 1989.

Brewer, Marilyn B., and Hewstone, Miles. "Introduction to this Volume." In *Self and Social Identity*, edited by Marilyn B. Brewer and Miles Hewstone, 3–4. Malden, MA: Blackwell, 2004.

Browne, Matthew, et al. "Intercultural Inquiry of Religion and Identity-Making at Carnegie Mellon University." Unpublished manuscript, last modified in 2003.

Brubaker, Rogers, and Frederick Cooper. "Beyond 'Identity.'" *Theory and Society* 29 (2000) 1–47.

Burke, Peter J., and Jan E Stets. *Identity Theory.* New York: Oxford University Press, 2009.

Chappell, David W. "Religious Identity and Openness in a Pluralistic World." *Buddhist-Christian Studies* 25 (2005) 9–14.

Charmaz, Kathy. *Constructing Grounded Theory: A Practical Guide through Qualitative Analysis.* Thousand Oaks, CA: Sage, 2006.

Chen, Guo-Ming. " ." In *Intercultural Communication: A Reader, 13th edition*, edited by Larry. A. Samovar et al., 95–103. Boston: Wadsworth, 2009.

Chia, M. T. Jack. "Buddhism in Singapore: A State of the Field Review." *Asian Culture* 33 (2009) 81–93.

———. "Teaching Dharma, Grooming Sangha: The Buddhist College of Singapore." *Sojourn* 24 (2009) 122–38.

Chiew, Seen Kong. "The Chinese in Singapore: From Colonial Times to the Present." In *Southeast Asian Chinese: The Socio-Cultural Dimension*, edited by Leo Suryadinata, 42–66. Singapore: Times Academic, 1995.

———. "Chinese Singaporeans: Three Decades of Progress and Changes." In *Ethnic Chinese in Singapore and Malaysia: A Dialogue between Tradition and Modernity*, edited by Leo Suryadinata, 11–44. Singapore: Times Academic, 2002.

Ching, Julia. *Chinese Religions.* Maryknoll, NY: Orbis, 1993.

Choong, Chee Pang. "Religious Composition of the Chinese in Singapore: Some Comments on the Census 2000." In *Ethnic Chinese in Singapore and Malaysia: A Dialogue between Tradition and Modernity*, edited by Leo Suryadinata, 325–36. Singapore: Times Academic, 2002.

Chua, Beng Huat. *Communitarian Ideology and Democracy in Singapore.* New York: Routledge, 1995.

———. "Foreword." In *The Scripting of a National History: Singapore and its Pasts*, edited by Lysa Hong & Jian Li Huang, ix–xi. Hong Kong: Hong Kong University Press, 2008.

———. "Racial-Singaporeans: Absence after the Hyphen." In *Southeast Asian Identities: Culture and the Politics of Representation in Indonesia, Malaysia, Singapore, and Thailand*, edited by Joel. S. Kahn, 28–50. Singapore: Institute of Southeast Asian Studies, 1998.

Clammer, John. "Chinese Ethnicity and Political Culture in Singapore." In *The Chinese in Southeast Asia, Vol. 2. Identity, Culture and Politics*, edited by Lee A. P. Gosling and Linda Y. C. Lim, 266–84. Singapore: Maruzen Asia, 1983.

———. "Religious Pluralism and Chinese Beliefs in Singapore." In *Chinese Beliefs and Practices in Southeast Asia*, edited by Cheu Hock Tong, 199–221. Petaling Jaya, Malaysia: Pelanduk, 1983.

Bibliography

Corbin, Juliet, and Anselm Strauss. *Basics of Qualitative Research: Techniques and Procedures for Developing Grounded Theory*. Thousand Oaks, CA: Sage, 2007.
Cote, James E., and Charles G. Levine. *Identity Formation, Agency and Culture: A Social Psychological Synthesis*. Mahwah, NJ: Lawrence Erlbaum, 2002.
Creswell, John W. *Qualitative Inquiry and Research Design: Choosing among Five Approaches*. Thousand Oaks, CA: Sage, 2007.
———. *Research Design: Qualitative, Quantitative, and Mixed Methods Approaches*. Thousand Oaks, CA: Sage, 2009.
Dashefsky, Arnold. "And the Search Goes On: The Meaning of Religio-Ethnic Identity and Identification." *Sociological Analysis*, 33 (1972) 239–45.
Deaux, Kay, and Peter Burke. "Bridging identities." *Social Psychology Quarterly* 73 (2010), 315–19.
DeBernardi, Jean. "Introduction." In *Cantonese Society in Hong Kong and Singapore: Gender, Religion, Medicine and Money. Essays by Marjorie Topley*, edited by Jean DeBernardi, 1–24. Hong Kong: Hong Kong University Press, 2011.
Denzin, Norman K., and Yvonna S Lincoln. *Strategies of Qualitative Inquiry*. Thousand Oaks, CA: Sage, 2008.
Durai, Jenanni. "Buddhist Groups Reach Out to Young People." http://eresources.nlb.gov.sg/newspapers/Digitised/Issue/straitstimes20110518-1.
Dykstra, Craig, and Dorothy C. Bass. "Foreword." In *Teaching and Christian Practices: Reshaping Faith and Learning*, edited by David. I. Smith and James K. A. Smith, vii–x. Grand Rapids, MI: Eerdmans, 2011.
Elliot, Alan J. A. *Chinese Spirit-Medium Cults in Singapore. Monographs on Social Anthropology No. 14*. London: The London School of Economics and Political Science, 1955.
Elmer, Duane H. *Cross-Cultural Servanthood: Serving the World in Christlike Humility*. Downers Grove, IL: InterVarsity, 2006.
Erikson, Erik H. *Childhood and Society*. New York: W. W. Norton, 1950.
———. *Identity: Youth and Crisis*. New York: W. W. Norton, 1968.
———. *Identity and the Life Cycle*. New York: W. W. Norton, 1959.
———. "The Problem of Ego Identity." *JAPA* IV (1956) 56–121.
Fisherman, Shraga. "Ego Identity and Spiritual Identity in Religiously Observant Adolescents in Israel." *Religious Education* 99 (2004) 371–84.
———. "Spiritual Identity in Israeli Religious Male Adolescents: Observations and Educational Implications." *Religious Education* 97 (2002) 61–79.
Flick, Uwe. *An Introduction to Qualitative Research*. Thousand Oaks, CA: Sage, 1998.
Freedman, Maurice. *The Study of Chinese Society*. Stanford, CA: Stanford University Press, 1979.
Gethin, Rupert. *The Foundations of Buddhism*. New York: OPUS, 1998.
Glaser, Barney G., Anselm L. Strauss. *The Discovery of Grounded Theory: Strategies for Qualitative Research*. New Brunswick, NJ: Aldine Transaction, 1999.
Gleason, Philip. "Identifying Identity: A Semantic History." *JAH* 69 (1983) 910–31.
Goh, Daniel P. S. "Chinese Religion and the Challenge of Modernity in Malaysia and Singapore: Syncretism, Hybridisation and Transfiguration." *AJSS* 37 (2009) 107–37.
Goh, Robbie B. H. "Christian Identities in Singapore: Religion, Race and Culture between State Controls and Transnational Flows." *JCG* 26 (2009) 1–23.
Goransson, Kristina. *The Binding Tie: Chinese Intergenerational Relations in Modern Singapore*. Honolulu: University of Hawaii Press, 2009.

Bibliography

Greenfield, Emily A., and Nadine F. Marks. "Religious Social Identity as an Explanatory Factor for Associations between more Frequent Formal Religious Participation and Psychological Wellbeing." *IJPR* 17 (2012) 245–59.
Hall, Stuart. "Introduction: Who Needs 'Identity?'" In *Questions of Cultural Identity*, edited by Stuart Hall and Paul du Gay, 1–17. Thousand Oaks, CA: Sage, 1996.
Hayward, R. David, et al. "Recollections of Childhood Religious Identity and Behavior as a Function of Adult Religiousness." *IJPR* 22 (2012) 79–88.
Heinze, Ruth-Inge. "The Dynamics of Chinese Religion: A Recent Case of Spirit Possession in Singapore." In *Chinese Beliefs and Practices in Southeast Asia*, edited by Cheu Hock Tong, 187–98. Petaling Jaya, Malaysia: Pelanduk, 1993.
Hiebert, Paul. "The Flaw of the Excluded Middle." *Missiology X* (1983), 35–47.
———. *Missiological Implications of Epistemological Shifts: Affirming Truth in a Modern/Postmodern World*. Harrisburg, PA: Trinity Press International, 1999.
Hiroshi, Maruyama. "Documents Used in Rituals of Merit in Taiwanese Daoism." In *Daoist Identity: History, Lineage, and Ritual*, edited by Livia Kohn and Harold D. Roth, 256–73. Honolulu: University of Hawaii Press, 2002.
Hogg, Michael A., and Dominic Abrams. "Social Identity and Social Cognition: Historical Background and Current Trends." In *Social Identity and Social Cognition*, edited by Dominic Abrams and Michael A. Hogg, 1–25. Malden, MA: Blackwell, 1999.
Hogg, Michael A., et al. "A Tale of Two Theories: A Critical Comparison of Identity Theory with Social Identity Theory." *SPQ* 58 (1995) 255–69.
Hong, Lysa, and Jian Li Huang. *The Scripting of a National History: Singapore and its Pasts*. Hong Kong: Hong Kong University Press, 2008.
Hopkins, Nick. "Religion and Social Capital: Identity Matters." *JCASP* 21 (2011) 528–40.
Hu, Shih. "Religion and Philosophy in Chinese History." In *Symposium on Chinese Culture*, edited by HengZhe Chen, 150–64. New York: Paragon, 1969.
Hue, Guan Thye. "Zhong hua chuan tong zong jiao xin yang nen de tui bian: Xin jia po de dao jiao he fo jiao yan jiu. The transformation of traditional Chinese religious beliefs in Southeast Asian Society–A Case Study of Taoism and Buddhism." PhD diss., Nanyang Technological University, 2011
Ichiko, Shiga. "Manifestations of Luzu in Modern Guangdong and Hong Kong: The Rise and Growth of Spirit-Writing Cults." In *Daoist Identity: History, Lineage, and Ritual*, edited by Livia Kohn and Harold D. Roth, 185–209. Honolulu: University of Hawaii Press, 2002.
Jarvis, Peter. *Human Learning*. New York: Routledge, 2006.
Jenkins, Peter. *The Next Christendom: The Coming of Global Christianity*. New York: Oxford, 2007.
Khor, Victor C. C., and Graeme Chapman. *A New Perspective on the Dao De Jing: Classic of Word and Integrity*. Petaling Jaya, Malaysia: Pelanduk, 2002.
King, Pamela E. "Religion and Identity: The Role of Ideological, Social, and Spiritual Contexts." *ADS* 7 (2003) 197–204.
Kluver, Randolf, and Ian Webber. "Patriotism and the Limits of Globalization: Renegotiating Citizenship in Singapore." *JCI* 27 (2003), 371–88.
Kohn, Livia, and Harold D. Roth. "Introduction." In *Daoist Identity: History, Lineage, and Ritual*, edited by Livia Kohn and Harold D. Roth, 1–22. Honolulu: University of Hawaii Press, 2002.
Kraft, Charles. *Christianity in Culture: A Study in Biblical Theologizing in Cross-Cultural Perspective*. Maryknoll, NY: Orbis, 2005.

Bibliography

Kroger, Jane. "Ego Identity Status Research in the New Millennium." *IJBD* 24 (2000) 145–48.
Kuah-Pearce, Khun Eng. *State, Society and Religious Engineering: Towards a Reformist Buddhism in Singapore*. Singapore: Eastern Universities Press, 2009.
Lagerwey, John. *Taoist Ritual in Chinese Society and History*. New York: MacMillan, 1983.
Lai, Ah Eng. "Conclusion". In *Religious Diversity in Singapore*, edited by Ah Eng Lai, 689–94. Singapore: Institute of Southeast Asian Studies, 2008.
———. "Introduction." In *Religious Diversity in Singapore*, edited by Ah Eng Lai, xliii–lix. Singapore: Institute of Southeast Asian Studies, 2008.
Lau, Henry H. T. "Buddhism and Youth in Singapore." *Ching Feng* XVI (1972), 101–03.
Lee, Chuek Yin et al. *Taoism: Outlines of a Chinese Religious Tradition*. Singapore: Taoist Federation, 1994.
Lee, Edwin. *The British as Rulers: Governing Multi-Racial Singapore, 1867–1914*. Singapore: Singapore University Press, 1991.
Lee, Y. M. "Buddhism and Chinese Culture: The Case Study of Guanyin Veneration." Paper presented at the International Conference on Religion and Culture, Chiang Mai, Thailand, June 2007.
Lian, Kwen Fee, and Chee Kiong Tong. "Constructing and Deconstructing Singapore Society." In *The Making of Singapore Sociology: Society and State*, edited by Chee Kiong Tong and Kwen Fee Lian, 1–20. Singapore: Times Academic, 2002.
Lim, Jessica. "NUS Orders Christian Group to Stop all Activities on Campus." http://www.straitstimes.com/BreakingNews/Singapore/Story/STIStory_769329.html.
Ling, Trevor. "Buddhism, Confucianism, and the Secular State in Singapore." Working Paper No. 79, National University of Singapore, 1987.
———. "Singapore: Buddhist Development in a Secular State." In *Buddhist Trends in Southeast Asia*, edited by Trevor Ling, 154–83. Singapore: Institute of Southeast Asian Studies, 1993.
Marcia, James E. "Development and Validation of Ego-Identity Status." *JPSP* 3 (1966) 551–58.
———. "Identity and Psychosocial Development in Adulthood." *Identity* 2 (2002) 7–28.
———. "The Identity Status Approach to the Study of Ego Identity Development." In *Self and Identity: Perspectives Across the Lifespan*, edited by Terry Honess and Krysia Yardley, 87–92. New York: Routledge, 1987.
Marshall, Catherine, and Gretchen B. Rossman. *Designing Qualitative Research*, 3rd ed. Thousand Oaks, CA: Sage, 1999.
Merriam, Sharan B. *Qualitative Research: A Guide to Design and Implementation*. San Francisco: Jossey-Bass, 2009.
Merriam, Sharan B., and Associates. *Non-Western Perspectives on Learning and Knowing*. Malabar, India: Krieger, 2007.
Mitchell, Donald W. *Buddhism: Introducing the Buddhist Experience*. New York: Oxford University Press, 2008.
Mol, Hans. *Identity and the Sacred*. New York: Free Press, 1976.
Mutalib, Hussein. "Singapore's Quest for a National Identity: The Triumphs and Trials of Government Policies." In *Imagining Singapore*, edited by Kah Choon Ban et al., 69–96. Singapore: Times Academic, 1992.
Ong, Y. D. *Buddhism in Singapore: A Short Narrative History*. Singapore: Skylark, 2005.
Operario, Don, and Susan T. Fiske. "Integrating Social Identity and Social Cognition: A Framework for Bridging Diverse Perspectives." In *Social Identity and Social*

Cognition, edited by Dominic Abrams and Michael A. Hogg, 26–54. Malden, MA: Blackwell, 1999.

Peek, Lori. "Becoming Muslim: The Development of a Religious Identity." *Sociology of Religion* 66 (2005) 215–42.

Piyasilo. *Buddhist Culture: An Observation of the Buddhist Situation in Malaysia and Singapore and a Suggestion*. Petaling Jaya, Malaysia: Friends of Buddhism Malaysia, 1988.

Potter, Garry, and Jose Lopez, eds. *After Postmodernism: An Introduction to Critical Realism*. London: Athlone, 2001.

See, Guat Kwee. "Building Bridges between Christians and Muslims." In *Religious Diversity in Singapore*, edited by Ah Eng, Lai, 668–88. Singapore: Institute of Southeast Asian Studies, 2008.

Singapore Department of Statistics. *Census of Population 2000*. https://www.singstat.gov.sg/publications/publications-and-papers/population#census_of_population_2000

———. *Census of Population 2010*. https://www.singstat.gov.sg/publications/publications-and-papers/population#census_of_population_2010.

Singapore Government. *Shared Values*. Singapore: Singapore National Printers, 1991.

Sinha, Vineeta. "'Hinduism' and 'Taoism' in Singapore: Seeing Points of Convergence." *JSEAS* 39 (2008) 123–47.

Smart, Ninian. *World Philosophies*, 2nd ed. New York: Routledge, 2008.

———. *Worldviews: Crosscultural Explorations of Human Beliefs*, 3rd ed. Saddle River, NJ: Prentice Hall, 2000

Starcher, Richard. *Africans in Pursuit of a Theological Doctorate: Doctoral Program Design in a Non-Western Context*. La Vergne, TN: Lambert Academic, 2010.

———. "Qualitative Research in Missiological Studies and Practice." *Dharma Deepika* 15.2 (2011) 54–63.

Stets, Jan E., and Peter J. Burke. "Identity Theory and Social Identity Theory." *Social Psychology Quarterly* 63 (2000) 224–37.

Stryker, Sheldon. "Identity Theory: Developments and Extensions." In *Self and Identity: Psychological Perspectives*, edited by Krisia Yardley and Terry Honess, 89–103. New York: John Wiley and Sons, 1987.

Stryker, Sheldon, and Peter J. Burke. "The Past, Present, and Future of an Identity Theory." *SPQ* 63 (2000) 284–97.

Stryker, Sheldon, and Richard T. Serpe. "Identity Salience and Psychological Centrality: Equivalent, Overlapping, or Complementary Concepts?" *SPQ* 57 (1994) 16–35.

Tajfel, Henri. *Human Groups and Social Categories: Studies in Social Psychology*. New York: Cambridge University Press, 1981.

———. "Introduction." In *Social Identity and Intergroup Relations*, edited by Henri Tajfel, 1–11. New York: Cambridge University Press, 1982.

Tamney, Joseph B. "A Sociological Approach to Buddhism in Singapore. *Ching Feng* 14.4 (1971) 153–56.

Tan, Charlene. "Creating 'Good Citizens' and Maintaining Religious Harmony in Singapore." *BJRE* 30 (2008) 133–42.

Tan, Chee Beng. "The Study of Chinese Religions in Southeast Asia: Some Views." In *Southeast Asian Chinese: The Socio-Cultural Dimension*, edited by Leo Suryadinata, 139–65. Singapore: Times Academic, 1995.

BIBLIOGRAPHY

Tan, Eugene K. B. "Keeping God in Place: The Management of Religion in Singapore. In *Religious Diversity in Singapore*, edited by Ah Eng, Lai, 55–82. Singapore: Institute of Southeast Asian Studies, 2008.

———. "Re-conceptualizing Chinese identity: The Politics of Chineseness in Singapore." In *Ethnic Chinese in Singapore and Malaysia: A Dialogue between Tradition and Modernity*, edited by Leo Suryadinata, 109–136. Singapore: Times Academic, 2002.

———. "Re-engaging Chinese-ness: Political, Economic and Cultural Imperatives of Nation Building in Singapore." *The China Quarterly* 175 (2003) 751–74.

Tay, C. N. "Guanyin: The Cult of Half Asia." In *Buddhism in Chinese Culture*, edited by Cheu Hock Teng, 149–86. Petaling Jaya, Malaysia: Pelanduk, 2000.

Terry, Deborah J., et al. "Group Membership, Social Identity, and Attitudes." In *Social Identity and Social Cognition*, edited by Dominic Abrams and Michael. A. Hogg, 280–314. Malden, MA: Blackwell, 1999.

Tham, Seong Chee. "Religious Influences and Impulses Impacting Singapore." In *Religious Diversity in Singapore*, edited by Ah Eng, Lai, 3–27. Singapore: Institute of Southeast Asian Studies, 2008.

Thera, Ananda M. "Buddha Dhamma and Singapore." *Ching Feng* XVI (1973) 142–51.

Thich, Nhat Hanh. *The Heart of Buddha's Teaching: Transforming Suffering into Peace, Joy, and Liberation*. New York: Broadway, 1998.

Thoits, Peggy A., and Lauren K. Virshup. "Me's and We's: Forms and Functions of Social Identities. In *Rutgers Series On Self And Social Identity: Vol. 1. Self and Identity: Fundamental Issues*, edited by Richard D. Ashmore and Lee Jussim, 106–36. New York: Oxford University Press, 1997.

Tong, Chee Kiong. *Rationalizing Religion: Religious Conversion, Revivalism and Competition in Singapore Society*. Boston: Brill, 2007.

———. "Religion." In *The Making of Singapore Sociology: Society and State* Chee, edited by Kiong Tong and Kwee Fee Lian, 370–413 Singapore: Times Academic, 2002.

Topley, Marjorie. "Chinese Religion and Religious Institutions in Singapore." In *Cantonese Society in Hong Kong and Singapore: Gender, Religion, Medicine and Money*, edited by Jean DeBernardi, 125–74. Hong Kong: Hong Kong University Press, 2011.

Tsomo, Karma Lekshe. "Creating Religious Identity." *Religion East and West* 9 (2009) 77–87.

Tulasiewicz, Witold, and Cho-Yee To. "Religion and Society." In *World Religions and Educational Practice*, edited by Witold Tulasiewicz and Cho-Yee To, 5–11. New York: Cassell, 1993.

Turnbull, Constance M. *A History of Modern Singapore, 1819–2005*. Singapore: National University of Singapore Press, 2009.

Turner, John C. "Towards a Cognitive Redefinition of the Social Group." In *Social Identity and Intergroup Relations*, edited by Henri Tajfel, 93–118. New York: Cambridge University Press, 1982.

Turner, John C., and Katherine J. Reynolds. "The Social Identity Perspective in Intergroup Relations: Theories, Themes, and Controversies." In *Self and Social Identity*, edited by Marilyn B. Brewer and Miles Hewstone, 259–77. Malden, MA: Blackwell, 2004.

Van Der Ven, Johannes A. "The Communicative Identity of the Local Church." In *Concilium: Catholic Identity. 1994/5*, edited by James. H. Provost and Knut Walf, 26–37. Maryknoll, NY: Orbis, 1994.

Volf, Miroslav. *Exclusion and Embrace: A Theological Exploration of Identity, Otherness, and Reconciliation*. Nashville: Abingdon, 1998.

Wang, Gungwu. *China and the Chinese Overseas.* Singapore: Eastern Universities Press, 2003.
Wee, Vivienne. "'Buddhism' in Singapore." In *Singapore: Society in Transition*, edited by Riaz Hassan, 154–88. New York: Oxford University Press, 1976.
Weigert, Andrew J., et al. *Society and Identity: Toward a Sociological Psychology.* New York: Cambridge University Press, 1986.
Weiss, Robert S. *Learning from Strangers: The Art and Method of Qualitative Interview Studies.* New York: Free Press, 1994.
Wenger, Etienne. *Communities of Practice: Learning, Meaning, and Identity.* New York: Cambridge University Press, 1998.
Williams, Paul. *Mahayana Buddhism: The Doctrinal Foundations*, 2nd ed. New York: Routledge, 2009.
Xu, Liying. "Daoist Temples in Modern City Life: The Singapore City God Temple." *Journal of Daoist Studies* 6 (2013) 114–42.
Yen, Fen. "Taoists and Buddhists still Biggest Group." http://eresources.nlb.gov.sg/newspapers/Digitised/Page/straitstimes20110113-2.1.8.
Ysseldyk, Renate, et al. "Religiosity as Identity: Toward an Understanding of Religion from a Social Identity Perspective." *Personality and Social Psychology Review* 14 (2010) 60–71.
Yu, Xue. "Merit Transfer and Life After Death in Buddhism." *Ching Feng* 4.1 (2003) 29–50.

www.ingramcontent.com/pod-product-compliance
Lightning Source LLC
Chambersburg PA
CBHW050810160426
43192CB00010B/1705